So how does assessment for learning fit into a lesson?

How can we fulfil the modern expectations of an OUTSTANDING learning for all?

The answer is the **Outstanding Lesson Framework**. A simple plan for lessons based on cutting down the workload and explaining the jargon. The structure ended up easy to follow and importantly to adapt to your own style. Use the framework and ideas in this book to gain confidence in your teaching and answer the age old question: **How do I plan an outstanding lesson?**

Outstanding Lessons made Simple

Dr. Richard Beard

authorHOUSE®

AuthorHouse™ UK
1663 Liberty Drive
Bloomington, IN 47403 USA
www.authorhouse.co.uk
Phone: 0800.197.4150

Published by AuthorHouse 12/18/2014

ISBN: 978-1-4918-8582-6 (sc)
ISBN: 978-1-4969-7962-9 (e)

Contents

ACKNOWLEDGEMENTS:
THE PEOPLE WHO MADE THIS BOOK POSSIBLE

Firstly, I would like to thank my wife Kate and my sons Scott, Richie and Ben. All have been a constant source of inspiration, support and grammatical correctness.

To my friends; Peter Rao for proof reading and suggesting ideas, and Anita Wyatt who completed my cover design. Both have been patient, engaging in numerous conversations in person and through e-mails whilst being so busy themselves (after all both are teachers).

Lastly, thanks goes to all the inspirational teachers I have watched and trained over the years seeking to make children's learning just as much exciting and intriguing as it is **EDUCATIONAL**.

THE AUTHOR

Dr Richard Beard started off as a science teacher at Codsall Community High School, Staffordshire, UK, and progressed to being an Advanced Skills Teacher (AST); gifted & talented co-ordinator; and science, technology, engineering, and mathematics (STEM) coordinator. This supportive role continued for four years and across all subjects within a mixture of age ranges as part of the Codsall High School Federation of Schools.

Throughout this period, Richard worked within an outstanding and innovative leadership team to help raise the quality of teaching rapidly from satisfactory (2007) to outstanding (2010). In three short years, the team had worked to complete a meteoric rise in the quality of teaching and learning.

Richard's work during this time, and in the present day, is heavily influenced by Assessment for Learning (AfL). He realised that training related to planning and the use of AfL lacked the simple approach. Confusion often reigned over what was good practice, especially in teachers just joining the profession.

From this, outstanding-lessons-made-simple.co.uk was created in the aim of promoting the simple approach: the Outstanding Lesson Framework. The Framework was designed to help teachers discover a simple and effective way to teach with the aim being that all teachers can deliver good and outstanding lessons all the time, not just in observations, with the simple backbone to good teaching: AfL.

At the present time, the Framework provides the basis for the improvement of the quality of teaching and learning across all schools within which Richard has worked. Richard now regularly delivers training on the framework and its use in improving the quality of teaching and learning across many different schools.

So, Can an Outstanding Lesson Be Simple?

Surprisingly, yes! A simple, straightforward approach can be taken in order to teach outstanding lessons in any subject. The Outstanding Lesson Framework can be used to plan and develop lessons with both a consistent quality and a varied approach. By initially attempting ideas from the Framework, and then using it as a guide to planning, your teaching can deliver an outstanding impact on you and your students' learning. The Outstanding Lesson Framework deciphers the outstanding lesson into bite-sized chunks, which are all intended to be engaging and inspiring for the students. The key themes throughout are independence, engagement, and challenge.

Each section of the Framework is described with a varied range of tried and tested techniques from which to choose. The Framework is essentially a tick list; although this does not mean that each section must be done in the order it is posted. In fact, you can mix it up and even allow the students to be in control. Throughout planning, the Outstanding Lesson Framework is designed to be a reference from which lessons can be planned and new ideas can be gained on how to carry out techniques in an outstanding way.

So, Why Should You Read On?

How many courses have we all been on where we have been inspired for the day? We often leave with a big smile spreading across our faces in anticipation of putting the ideas into practice the very next day. We then go back to our classroom and place the folder on a shelf. The day-to-day activities within a school continue and alas, the folder is never to see the light of day again. Even worse, we often struggle to remember what practical ideas we got from this course, and if we do remember, it is only one, or maybe two, techniques at best.

The aim of this book is to change all that and provide a one-stop shop to plan outstanding lessons consistently and often with few resources. Outstanding learning is not just about the resources. It is about the way they are used. In this book, we will explain various different ways to use everyday techniques practically. These are often written throughout the book as "quick tips", which give information relating to each teaching idea. Quick tips can be anything from apps you can use with a teaching idea, a website with useful features, resource-free ways of using the methods, and differentiation techniques for the teaching idea in question.

So, from this point forward, everything you see will be practical whether for low-, middle-, or high-ability students. It doesn't matter what stage you are at, start dreaming about how you can plan for an outstanding lesson where you and the children have a great big smile at the end. Enough of the introduction—let's get stuck in!

The Outstanding Lesson Framework

Where Has This Come From?

As with all ideas, the Framework started from a conversation in a training session. A colleague was very tired and confused at the end of the training session and asked,

"This is all well and good, and I know there are loads of resources, but it is all too confusing. There are so many different ways to teach. Why can't we just have something simple?"

So, a Framework was initially roughly planned on a piece of scrap paper, which was then developed over time into the Outstanding Lesson Framework.

The Framework is designed to be as simple as possible. It is not intended to be restrictive and as such, there are no timings, as well, the different parts can be jumbled up into different orders. It is, however, essentially a simple starting place to design lessons that have all of the essential elements to cement outstanding learning. The ingenuity and individualism of all teachers can flourish by adapting these different techniques. In fact, you can jumble up the Framework to whatever way you see fit for your style and for your students.

The arrows in the Framework are essentially a flow chart. For example, the Framework shows that after the starter activity is completed, the teacher can use an engaging questioning technique to glean some ideas from the students. This can also be done during the actual teaching sequence when the new knowledge is delivered.

Of particular importance, is the chance to be independent and collaborate using differentiated tasks and peer-, or self-assessment, strategies. This opportunity is described on the right of the Framework, allowing for students to work for an extended period of time in groups and/or independently. In order for this to happen, it is essential that the work is set at the right level of challenge. The work must be engaging, through being difficult enough to present a challenge, but not too difficult so that it turns the students off. Students can work together to solve problems and create solutions which are key in any subject.

This is a small introduction to whet the appetite, which will go into further detail throughout the different chapters of the book. You can either read the book from front to back or choose where to start. The overall structure of the book is such that teachers can save time by quickly going to their favoured sections because, as we all know, no teacher has very much time.

Outstanding
Lesson Framework

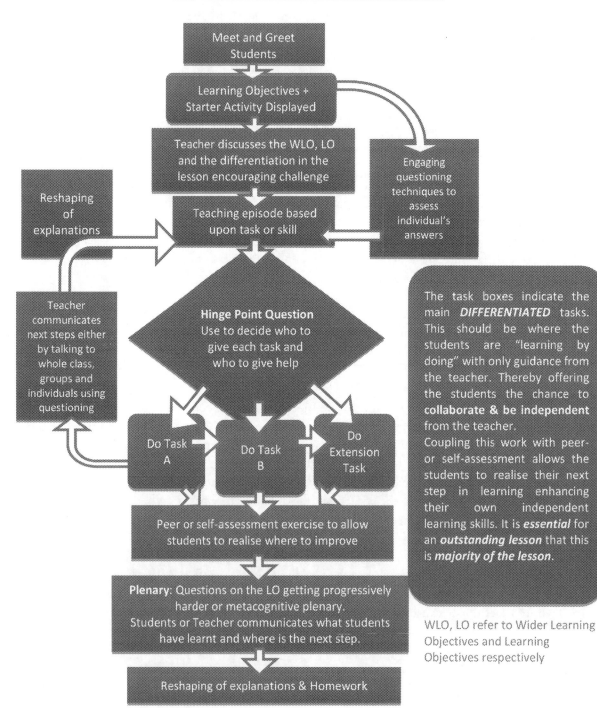

Meet and Greet Students

Learning Objectives + Starter Activity Displayed

Teacher discusses the WLO, LO and the differentiation in the lesson encouraging challenge

Engaging questioning techniques to assess individual's answers

Reshaping of explanations

Teaching episode based upon task or skill

Teacher communicates next steps either by talking to whole class, groups and individuals using questioning

Hinge Point Question
Use to decide who to give each task and who to give help

Do Task A

Do Task B

Do Extension Task

The task boxes indicate the main *DIFFERENTIATED* tasks. This should be where the students are "learning by doing" with only guidance from the teacher. Thereby offering the students the chance to **collaborate & be independent** from the teacher.
Coupling this work with peer- or self-assessment allows the students to realise their next step in learning enhancing their own independent learning skills. It is *essential* for an *outstanding lesson* that this is *majority of the lesson*.

Peer or self-assessment exercise to allow students to realise where to improve

Plenary: Questions on the LO getting progressively harder or metacognitive plenary.
Students or Teacher communicates what students have learnt and where is the next step.

WLO, LO refer to Wider Learning Objectives and Learning Objectives respectively

Reshaping of explanations & Homework

8

How Can You Use the Framework?

Each section of the lesson is described so that you can jump straight to the part you're interested in, in order to save time. This book is not necessarily designed to be read from front to back, but to be dipped in and out of to find your area of interest. Hopefully, this sounds simple; after all, that's the point.

The Framework can be used in different ways depending on your stage in your teaching career. In the next two sections, take a look at the pathways and helpful hints for those that are new to the teaching profession, or school leaders:

New to the Teaching Profession

Starting out in teaching is a very difficult process, and many ideas are thrown at a new teacher; so pick an area to focus on first. Usually, this follows the chronology of the Framework. For example, begin with learning objectives and success criteria progressing to teaching techniques, engaging questioning, and so on.

Once you have chosen an area, read the explanation at the beginning of the chapter and choose some ideas to try out. Carry on with this until you feel comfortable and confident and know what works. After all, no idea works for everybody in the way it is written. The best teachers change the ideas subtly to work for them and their class.

Also, beware of spreading yourself too thin and attempting to master all of the techniques at once. Instead, pick a focus for your lessons from the Framework, such as differentiated tasks, plenaries, or hinge point questions. Just make sure the focus is suited to you and to what you need to develop. If you go too quickly, you will fulfil the role of "jack of all trades and master of none".

School Leaders', Heads of Departments', and/or Faculties' Priorities

It is no surprise that quality of teaching is the top priority in any forward-thinking school. Any school is brought forward by the hardworking, innovative teachers at the chalkboard and leaders who are always clear on what they want. The expectations of teachers must be clear and transparent from the beginning, and all teachers must be part of the planning for the future.

The Framework can be used to plan for the future and iron out these expectations in a coherent manner. Listed below are a few ideas on getting the process started:

1. Before the whole school introduction of the Framework, consult a small working party.
   ◦ Draw together the working party, including one teacher from each department.
   ◦ Get the working party to try the Framework and give feedback to each other.
   ◦ Tailor the order/wordings if necessary for your school.
   ◦ Deliver training for the whole school on the structure and its elements.
2. Include the newly tailored Framework in the school's teaching and learning policy.
3. Make the Framework public, either on your website, intranet, or virtual learning environment (VLE) for all staff.
4. Give physical copies to everybody in one or all of these forms:
   ◦ a copy in each teacher's planner;
   ◦ laminated A3 versions for ease of use in classrooms;
   ◦ learning walls in each classroom that incorporate the Framework amongst many other ideas.

The Framework has made a large impact at many different schools, and as such, there are very positive experiences summarised above. If you would like to take your school on a similar journey, please visit www.outstanding-lessons-made-simple.co.uk or contact feedback@outstanding-lessons-made-simple.co.uk for training materials and editable copies of the Framework.

Lesson Observation Feedback

Determine your focus in your department by using the different areas of the Framework as a diagnostic tool in lesson observation feedback. It is very easy to use the Framework as a discussion piece for feedback and subsequent development. For example:

Lead: "You differentiated well with excellent resources. How did you find out where everyone was at in your lesson so you could give them the right task for their level?"

Teacher: "I used their data to set the work."

Lead: "Did that work for every student?"

Teacher: "No, there were a couple of students who finished very quickly, and I didn't expect that."

Lead: "Look at the Framework for a lesson. What could you have developed to make sure these students had the correctly levelled work?"

Teacher: "Hinge point questions, but I'm not sure how to do it effectively."

This begins a focused discussion between the relevant lead and the teacher, including reflection for both parties. The more reflective teachers are, the more their teaching improves. This also allows them to come up with their own answers and develop their own practices, which is the art of a good teacher.

Leading for Change

Each head of department or school recognises the teaching areas that need development. However, sometimes this can be not clearly defined or linked to training. Each chapter/section can also be used as a basis for the lead of the department/school to gain ideas. These ideas can be used to help and develop teaching with a clear focus on outcomes. There are many more, however, here are three examples:

- Area for development: challenge
  - Framework leads us to two clearly defined areas: learning objectives and differentiation.
- Area for development: clear assessment within lessons
  - Framework leads us to develop training on hinge point questions and peer-/self-assessment techniques.
- Area for development: independent students
  - Framework leads us to differentiation techniques and peer-/self-assessment techniques.

Self-Managers

For teaching to be strong across a school, all teachers must be self-managers and be able to assess their own strengths and weaknesses. In a forward-thinking environment, members of staff will run training in these areas and train themselves and others to be experts. The Framework allows these areas to be clearly defined in a visual context and used as diagnostic tools for teachers to identify their individual needs. This then feeds forward into the development of training across the faculty or school.

Key Themes of the Outstanding Lesson Framework

As well as the Framework itself, there are key themes which are common in all outstanding lessons, such as relationships, behaviour, and consistency. All are related to each other in some way and all are essential in achieving greater independence for students.

In the next two chapters, "Key Themes of The Outstanding Lesson Framework" and "Different Sections of the Outstanding Lesson Framework", these themes will be explained in combination with a brief description of each part of the Framework itself. The intention is that by reading these brief introductions, you can save time by picking and choosing what areas you wish to concentrate upon first.

The general themes will not be given explicit chapters, but as with an outstanding lesson, they are interlaced throughout the book. For example: when developing relationships, it is essential that praise heavily outweighs criticism; or in other words, the carrot outweighs the stick. As teaching ideas are explained, ideas on how to praise the students will be given as part of the description to promote widespread and effective praise.

Relationships

All of us want to be that inspiring teacher that children will talk about when they're older. My own teaching passions were gained from the history lessons I enjoyed at school. The inspiring teacher was Mr Bagshaw, a fantastic teacher who never failed to make us smile. At the same time, all of us learned so much about history. I still have a love of history to this day thanks to Mr Bagshaw.

This nostalgic story was included because good relationships with students are a key aspect of outstanding learning. Put simply, if there is not a good relationship, the outstanding lesson is just not possible. For students to thrive, it is the job of the teacher to develop them as independent students who can survive and flourish in the busy commercial world of today. However, at the stage at which children are taught, we are only starting them on this journey of independence. Teachers need to gradually develop their students by allowing them to attempt tasks where they have some responsibility or choice. On the flip side, students will only trust their teacher if they have a good relationship. They need to know that the teacher is acting in their best interest, and that they will be safe from bullying or distress. Observers often write the following on feedback or words to that effect: "Students are engaged, resilient, and thrive on challenge."

This observation will never occur unless you have a good relationship with your students. It is amazing to see the difference in effort between students who are inspired and respect their teachers, compared with those who are indifferent or not bothered.

Consistency

I know this may be like teaching a teacher to suck eggs; however, it is very important. Imagine lessons were done every day without the elements of the Outstanding Lesson Framework, such as engaging questioning, assessment, and differentiation. An observation then came along, and you tried to tick boxes by adding these elements. Do you think it will work?

In most cases, it just won't work. Children are shrewd and can spot when it is just a performance for observers. They can also tell when a good teacher is just adding a bit more panache to their normal everyday teaching for the observer. If this is done, the students will usually answer positively, much like below:

Observer: "Is this a typical or normal lesson? Does the teacher always find out what you have learned?"

Student: "Yes, our teacher always tries to find out what we've learned, usually with mini-whiteboards."

So the lesson for the teacher is to use as many effective techniques as possible in normal everyday lessons. It will get the students used to a reflective and challenging approach, thereby fostering independence. This means that during observations, the students will just treat it like a normal lesson. They will progress in the same outstanding way as always.

Remember, this doesn't mean glitz and glamour have to be put into every single lesson. There are just not enough hours in the days to do that. Just use the techniques in the book that fulfil the different sections of pedagogy, and do those that take the least preparation, the least hours, and get the most effective outcomes.

Consider assessment or differentiation:

1. Assessment with hinge point questions using the student's fingers, or getting out mini-whiteboards, will take hardly any preparation so they can be done regularly with ease and require little planning.
2. Differentiating by giving students different roles can also be done with very little preparation. For more information on both those techniques, read on or jump straight to the relevant chapter.

Assessment for Learning (Adaptive Assessment)

Formative assessment, or Assessment for Learning (AfL), which is now termed in some areas as "adaptive assessment", flows throughout the Framework, and hence, is an important focus throughout this book. The definition of Assessment for Learning is as follows:

> *Assessment for learning is any assessment for which the first priority in its design and practice is to serve the purpose of promoting pupils' learning. An assessment activity can help learning if it provides information to be used as feedback by teachers, and by their pupils, in assessing themselves and each other to modify the teaching and learning activities in which they are engaged. Such assessment becomes 'formative assessment' when the evidence is actually used to adapt the teaching work to meet learning needs.*

> *(Black, Harrison, Lee, Marshall & Wiliam 2002)*

Simply put, it is some form of assessment that leads to teachers or students acting upon the results. The teacher, in essence, changes their actions to develop the learning based on what they see or hear from the students.

In terms of a lesson, it means that the teacher uses assessment to establish where the students are in their learning. The teacher knows where the students' learning is going and works out how to get it there and is, therefore, adaptive. It also means that the students can recognise where they are at in their learning, where they are going, and how they are going to get there. This enhances the student's independent learning abilities and allows them to think on their feet in any situation, which is a skill all industry desires in our children.

A simple example is a teacher noticing that a student does not understand how to add tens and units together after they have taught the whole class. They then go to the student and describe it in a different way which is referred to throughout the Framework as "reshaping learning".

There are five areas of assessment for learning which the Framework is designed to develop:

1. *Clarifying, understanding, and sharing learning objectives/intentions*
2. *Engineering effective classroom discussions, tasks, and activities that elicit evidence of learning: classroom discourse and interactive whole-class teaching*
3. *Providing feedback that moves students forward*
4. *Activating students as learning resources for one another: collaborative learning, reciprocal teaching, peer-assessment*
5. *Activating students as owners of their own learning: metacognition, motivation, interest, attribution, self-assessment*

(Wiliam & Thompson 2007)

Each area of AfL is delivered through the Framework at different points. In each chapter, different strategies for carrying out AfL will be described as well as how to carry them out in a classroom context. The next diagram features the areas in which AfL is catered for throughout the Outstanding Lesson Framework.

As can be seen, AfL is for a specific purpose to move learning and students forward. It is not just a tick box, and needs to be done regularly to make an impact on learning. This is why it is so essential to an outstanding lesson.

Outstanding
Lesson Framework

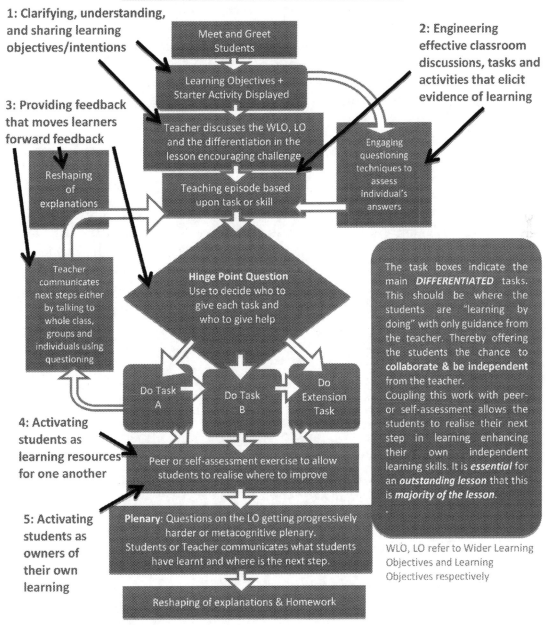

1: Clarifying, understanding, and sharing learning objectives/intentions

Meet and Greet Students

Learning Objectives + Starter Activity Displayed

3: Providing feedback that moves learners forward feedback

Teacher discusses the WLO, LO and the differentiation in the lesson encouraging challenge

Reshaping of explanations

Teaching episode based upon task or skill

Teacher communicates next steps either by talking to whole class, groups and individuals using questioning

Hinge Point Question
Use to decide who to give each task and who to give help

2: Engineering effective classroom discussions, tasks and activities that elicit evidence of learning

Engaging questioning techniques to assess individual's answers

The task boxes indicate the main *DIFFERENTIATED* tasks. This should be where the students are "learning by doing" with only guidance from the teacher. Thereby offering the students the chance to **collaborate & be independent** from the teacher.
Coupling this work with peer- or self-assessment allows the students to realise their next step in learning enhancing their own independent learning skills. It is *essential* for an *outstanding lesson* that this is *majority of the lesson.*

Do Task A

Do Task B

Do Extension Task

4: Activating students as learning resources for one another

Peer or self-assessment exercise to allow students to realise where to improve

5: Activating students as owners of their own learning

Plenary: Questions on the LO getting progressively harder or metacognitive plenary.
Students or Teacher communicates what students have learnt and where is the next step.

WLO, LO refer to Wider Learning Objectives and Learning Objectives respectively

Reshaping of explanations & Homework

AfL is the lifeblood of the framework and mentioned throughout.

Behaviour Management

I have had many conversations with different teachers, and most will agree that good teaching means less need for classic behaviour management. Therefore, I will not discuss in detail behaviour management in this book. However, there will be numerous examples discussed that have behavioural slants, which are mainly all talking about a simple carrot-and-stick approach with a real application of engagement. If students are engaged through exciting teaching methodology, then much disruptive behaviour will just not arise. Remember, those who are engaged and enjoy their learning present less behavioural issues. Engagement is variety, so vary your ideas all the time.

Pace

Every outstanding lesson has to be set at a good pace, in which the students must be challenged, but not given too little time to complete the task. This is one of the hardest skills of a teacher because it all depends upon the teacher's judgement of the students' abilities and how long they will take to complete each task. There are just so many different factors to take into account that it can be very difficult at times. There are tips all the way through the book about setting the timings for different tasks, so look out for them. Here, we will look at some general tips for pace that should keep you in good stead.

- **Clocks—Do We Need Them?**
  - Keep the children guessing on timings; don't help them out by having a clock on the wall. It can be a distraction they don't need and some will end up clock watching and not focusing on their work.

- **Teacher Time**
  - Teachers control the time and set the time limits. Therefore, teachers can make it last as long or as short as they wish, (e.g. if you say two minutes, it doesn't have to be two minutes; it may be one minute thirty seconds or three minutes). Trust me, the students will not look at their watches; they will just feel the pace of the lesson due to the clear, pacey timings.

- **Regular Reminders**
  - Remind the students regularly on the time left. This can be done either by telling the students or by different applications that ring out bells or chimes at set intervals. The pace will increase if the students know there are one or two minutes left in a ten-minute project. It will not increase if they have no awareness.

- **Competition**
  - Where appropriate, introduce some form of friendly competition to encourage challenge. There are many examples throughout the book to get stuck into but the main principle is always the same: if tasks are competitive, then time, in the students' eyes, will go faster and the lesson will be pacier.

<table>
<tr>
<td>Quick
tip</td>
<td>Can you beat Google? This is a quick tip to get the pace going and the excitement raised immediately. Lay a sportsman bet: "Can you find the answer before I find it on Google? Stop me if you know. Go!" The students will rush to do it all in the course of a great bit of friendly competition to get the pace of the lesson up.</td>
</tr>
</table>

Voice and the Movement within the Classroom

A great teacher always keeps the class guessing. What is he or she going to do next? What kind of learning is going to happen today? You know you are on the right lines in terms of teaching if the children enter in an excited way and ask you what they are doing today. This is because they are looking forward to the lesson because they can't predict what is going to happen. Throughout the book engagement is referred to as "variety", and voice and movement have differing elements of variety in the toolkit of an outstanding teacher which we describe below.

Think back to when you were at school. Did you listen to the teachers who were slow and meandering, or the ones who got straight to the point but remained clear? I was the latter. So, how do you become well-paced and to the point? A few points:

- **Eye Contact**
  - Eye contact is a way to make children feel like they are involved. Look at them, although it doesn't have to be for long. It is not the intention to make students feel uncomfortable. The aim is just for students to know that the teacher recognises them so that they feel safe and part of the lesson. No one is ignored in an outstanding lesson, and there are no black sheep.

- **Movement**
  - Look around whilst teaching and try to catch student's eyes as above. Notice the students moving their heads subtly which allows the teacher to know who is listening. This also indicates that their attention is high because they are actively following. Use this information to guide your movements around the class. If you notice anyone lacking attention, move generally in that direction and start engaging with those students, usually through questioning.

- **Tempo**
  - When the lesson is nearing the exciting part, emphasise by changing your pitch. Introduce the lesson like a film trailer, making it exciting and relevant. Speed up that little bit, not too fast, but enough for the students to know something has changed. This signals "we're getting exciting now".

- **Pitch**
  - Change the pitch when the important keyword or sentence is being mentioned. It is up to the teacher how much the pitch varies.

- **Volume**
  - When speaking to a class, try to raise the volume when nearing a point that is very important; however, always remember not to shout.

The art is to combine all of these at key points in the lesson raising the tempo, volume, and pitch all at the same time. Students will be attentive in a way that they never were before. Keep at it, because this is a constantly practiced skill of which we all need to be aware.

Have You Practiced This Type of Lesson Before?

If you have a lesson observation, practice the style of lesson with a similar group, if possible. Never go into it cold. Make sure all of the techniques have been practiced before. Making sure the techniques are well practiced also gives you the chance to find out if they need tweaking. It helps by reflecting and using some simple questions:

- Did they learn something new?
- Are the timings realistic?
- Is there appropriate challenge? Do they find it thought provoking but doable?
- Did I find out everyone's level of understanding?
- Did the students already know what they were meant to learn?
- Do the students know they progressed?
- Do the students seem engaged and interested?
- Was it learning led or teacher led? Did they do most of the work?
- Was it pacey?

To achieve all of this may sound simple, but all teachers know it is not. The students must be trained to learn in this way. Not all students are natural learners. They may need to be encouraged to use inquisitive skills and flourish with a challenge.

By following the Framework and using the techniques in a varied (different techniques each lesson) and consistent way (in your own style), all of the above aims can be achieved.

Different Sections of the Outstanding Lesson Framework

From now on, chapters will be referred to for each section of the Framework for clarity and ease of navigation. To allow the choice of where you would like to read first (if you are skimming), each section of the Framework is briefly described to help you navigate to your area of choice simply and quickly.

Chapter 1:

The Meet-and-Greet

Meet and Greet Students

The first part of any lesson is the meet-and-greet where the students are welcomed. This may sound simple, but here we discuss how to get the most effective outcomes out of the meet-and-greet while students are coming in from their daily routines. During this time the teacher is noticing some really important behaviour that could affect the lesson. It also means they are there to encourage good behaviour and set the scene for the lesson immediately. By observing and being part of their entrance, poor behaviour and any possible issues that may result could be resolved straight away.

Put simply, you get to know your students if you stand at the door and ask those simple words:

"How are you? Have you had a good day?"

These words can start the lesson off in a real positive fashion and allows an immediate opportunity to see where intervention is needed.

In this chapter, we will discuss ways to start the lesson, including how to multitask—meeting and greeting whilst at the same time getting the learning initiated. Important time is used here to get to know the students which, as discussed, are integral to behaviour management, and so, learning.

Chapter 2:

Learning Objectives and Starters

> **Learning Objectives +**
> **Starter Activity Displayed**

This chapter is focused on the challenges relating to engaging students and on delivering effective starter activities. Many teachers teach five or more lessons a day, so how can teachers stand there each lesson meeting and greeting whilst having to write learning objectives on the whiteboard and doing a starter activity? This is multitasking at its best; and in this chapter, the simple answers are provided.

There are many different ways of sharing learning objectives, writing learning objectives and awesome starters. Here the simple starters are explained, and learning objectives demystified. All techniques described are engaging and easy to get started. This often means without any help from the teacher. So to get your lesson started, read into this chapter.

Chapter 3:

Encouraging Challenge by Sharing of Differentiated Learning Objectives (LO) and Wider Learning Objectives (WLO)

> **Teacher discusses the WLO, LO, and the differentiation in the lesson encouraging challenge**

This phase is incredibly important because this is where challenge is promoted. Wider learning objectives (WLO) are also included in a general context. All WLO in this book are based on:

- ○ Numeracy
- ○ Literacy
- ○ Personal learning and thinking skills (PLTS)
- ○ Personal, social, health, and economic education (PSHEE)
- ○ Information technology (IT)

It is essential in the current educational climate that literacy and numeracy are in all lessons. So, can every lesson have some form of literacy or numeracy slant? Of course they can and in a simple way. For example with literacy, we all use keywords and sentences orally, or in the written form, thereby, every lesson can have some form of literacy objective. Many ideas for delivering these cross-curricular slants will be described in this chapter.

As well as cross-curricular learning, it is also vital that all students are challenged in lessons so they can progress as far as possible. Some will move from; others from; and others from so all are learning to their utmost potential in your lessons. With that in mind, observers often ask students:

- ○ "What are you learning today?"
- ○ "Do you feel challenged in this lesson?"
- ○ "What is the next step in your learning?"
- ○ "What are you going to learn next?"

Students who can answer these questions are aided by having clear differentiated learning objectives and success criteria. Learning objectives in conjunction with success criteria are then used to design tasks which students can be directed to or through their own choice. This means a selection of the following can be given:

- Subtly different tasks allowing them to reach very similar objectives/success criteria
- Very different tasks linked to clear differentiated learning objectives/success criteria
- Different roles within the lesson
- Different levels for each student to aim at (this is essentially differentiation by outcome)

The whole lesson and the challenge within it, depends upon the learning objectives. So, in this chapter we will discuss how to write LOs to encourage challenge and celebrate it in conjunction with an engaging starter or a hook.

Chapter 4:

Teaching Period Based Upon a Task and/or a Skill

> **Teaching episode based
> upon task or skill**

Essentially, all ideas in this book can be used to teach. So, in this section we discuss different engaging techniques and strategies with which to teach. The chapter is deliberately not prescriptive in what you teach or how long it takes, however bear in mind, in an outstanding lesson, the teaching has to be at a minimum. This minimum can be different for different ages and abilities. A seven-year-old, for example, won't necessarily be as classically independent as a sixteen-year-old.

But what is independent learning? Well, here's one of the many definitions out there, although there are many: "The ability to take charge of one's learning" (H. Holec 1981). In practical terms, developing students who take charge of their learning are engaged in a challenging process, which doesn't happen overnight. For students to be independent in a lesson, traditional didactic teaching must be at a minimum level. Generally, aim to be at the whiteboard in front of the students for only 10 to 20 per cent of your lesson for the greatest learning to take place.

For a lesson to be successful with the teacher only being at the whiteboard for 10 to 20 per cent of the time, preparation is key. The design of engaging teaching episodes that give the opportunity for questions and exploration are essential. In some cases, students may well have some control over their own learning, however, the teacher still designs the process.

This chapter will give many examples of engaging teaching techniques often with a practical, independent learning style. This will allow students to be directed onto the main tasks, allowing more skills to be practiced in the lesson.

Chapter 5:

Engaging Questioning Techniques

> **Engaging questioning techniques to assess individual's answers**

An outstanding lesson has a group of children that are reflective, questioning and resilient to challenge. In this section, engaging questioning techniques are discussed and information is given on how to encourage students to ask questions. This develops their inquisitive nature and makes them excited about attempting more challenging work. Remember, being inquisitive is not always innate; it can, however, be nurtured and facilitated over time. It is the simplest way to get students laughing and questioning the teacher and each other.

Assessment will be discussed all the way through this book as it is integral to improving learning. Assessment allows the teacher to know what the students have learned and intervene to allow them to move on to the next stage. Strictly speaking, engaging questioning techniques only allow students to move forward on an individual basis and not the whole class. So, techniques to question and engage individuals are important, but they don't allow the teacher to know where everyone is in terms of learning. There are lots of techniques to engage and challenge students through questioning but read on for whole-class assessment.

Chapter 6:

Hinge Point Questioning aka Adaptive Assessment

Hinge Point Question:
Use to decide who to
give each task and
who to give help.

When teachers assess, the most popular technique is the simple question + answer (Q+A). One of the most common reasons for poor progress in learning is the lack of whole-class assessment and the failure of the teacher to act upon that assessment to help students. Put simply, did they realise that certain students were struggling? Did they then go to help? Did they reshape their explanations so the student could move on? Imagine the following situation where a teacher thought that this simple Q+A covers this:

"I (teacher) thought my assessment was good; I went around asking students and finding out what everybody knew!"

This works with a class of ten students, which very few of us have; however, it is practically impossible with a class of thirty students, which most of us have.

Let's put this into numbers with a class of thirty students in a sixty-minute lesson:

- No traditional teaching at the front means you have sixty minutes to speak to students and assess individually.
- Sixty minutes ÷ thirty students = two minutes per student to discuss the learning.

Doesn't sound like much does it? So imagine a more normal lesson:

- Teacher taught for ten minutes, leaving fifty minutes for individual assessment.
- Fifty minutes ÷ thirty students = 1.6 minutes per student.

Now let's get close to everyday reality of a teacher:

- Takes students five minutes to settle in and five minutes at least to pack away.
- Teacher teaches for ten minutes, leaving forty minutes to individually assess.
- Forty minutes ÷ thirty students = 1.3 minutes per student.

Looking at these timings, it is clear that teachers would have to be very efficient to reach every student on each example. The reality is that someone will be missed if only individual Q+A is used, and students who need help the most will likely be missed. This student is almost always the quietest learner who can be lazy, and/or very shy, or lack confidence. So this section discusses essential hinge point assessment of the whole class so the teacher knows where all students are at in their learning and how to intervene effectively.

The following key questions are considered:

- "How can I find out where all the class is in one to two minutes?"
- "What are the logistics of designing a good hinge point question?"
- "How can I design a question that allows the students to either choose or be given a differentiated task?"
- "How can I stop copying or make it more overt so I can see it?"

This chapter will answer all these queries and provide practical ideas on how to ask the questions. Advice will be given on how to organise the questioning with the resources. At the same time advice will be given on how to use hinge point questions whilst avoiding students copying each other by noticing it and intervening.

Chapter 7:

Designing Engaging Differentiated Tasks

To reach outstanding learning in a lesson, it is important to give a significant proportion, anywhere from 80 to 100 per cent of the lesson time, for students to be engaged in independent learning. In this time, students are expected to develop some form of independence usually by working collaboratively in groups or pairs. This is designed in such a way that it promotes reflection and normally has a problem solving element.

In the Outstanding Lesson Framework, it indicates three different tasks; however, this is up to the teacher. At this point, the real aim is to make sure that the learning is differentiated so that all students learn to their potential, despite their different abilities.

This can be done not only by giving different tasks tailored to their ability, but by allocating different roles or starting points.

So even though there are three boxes, this is an open area for overt differentiated approaches. For example, there can be two, three, four, five, or more different tasks or roles if you want. It all depends on the complexity of the planning. By making this section take the most time, it allows the teacher to go round questioning and speaking to students. This allows the students to fill their own gaps in learning and flourish in an independent setting. The teacher then naturally reshapes explanations through conversations, thus moving students forward. In simple terms, just walk around the class and find out what they are doing and how to help.

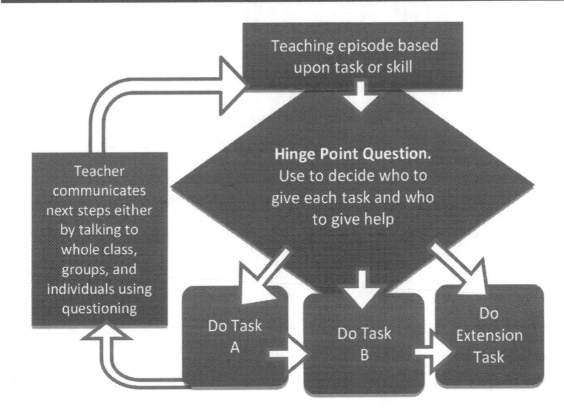

Take a look at larger sections of the Framework (above), which has many parts grouped together. This illustrates that the teacher realises through questioning that there are students who do not understand the learning aims. The outstanding teacher's role is to then teach in a different way and ask another hinge point question to redeliver a differentiated task as in the following section. This moves the students forward. In other words, the student's learning progresses. This is a classic example of how in-class assessment should be done; the teacher is using assessment to deliver the right work so the student can move on with their learning.

Go through this chapter to explore a myriad of differentiated processes. All of these teaching ideas will allow students to access different paths based upon their ability. Many teachers just don't have the time to create different tasks and resources. Therefore, this chapter will also focus on differentiation that requires the least preparation and in some cases no preparation at all.

Chapter 8:

Self—and Peer-Assessment

Peer or self-assessment exercises to allow
students to realise where to improve.

Self—or peer-assessment exercises are essential in cementing the independent nature of a student's learning. In the Framework, it is after the differentiated tasks. However, this can be placed in different parts of the lesson or revisited throughout. This is always recommended because this type of assessment allows students to reflect on their work and seek areas in which to improve.

In terms of observations, it is good for teachers to know that the observer will always want to find out from the students what they know and how to improve. Self—or peer-assessment allows the students to gain confidence in their ability, which is something observers wish to see. In time, this develops their independence by giving them the ability to reflect on their learning.

All self—or peer-assessment in this chapter is deep and thought provoking for the students as well as being simple to carry out. All ideas allow students to develop their answers with clear guidance and structure, thereby facilitating outstanding progress and realising the potential of each individual student.

Chapter 9:

Plenaries and Assessment

> Plenary: Questions on the learning objectives getting progressively harder or a metacognitive plenary.
>
> Students or teacher communicates what students have learnt and where the next step lies.

At the end of the lesson time, management is always a big factor. So ask yourself this while planning:

- How can I assess them quickly?
- What do I base my plenary on?
- How long will I realistically need?

These questions always lead to teacher reflection and a clear way forward in planning. The answers are again, straight forward and essential for outstanding learning, and so, progress. Both teacher and student need to know where they are in terms of their learning and where they need to improve. This means that the students will realise that they have progressed. Put simply, they are walking out knowing something or being able to do something they could not do when they first walked in.

The easiest way to facilitate this is the plenary, which either involves quickly assessing the students and informing them of their successes, or allowing them to assess their own progress (self-/peer-assessment or metacognition). Here it will also allow conversations with those few who still need a little guidance and haven't quite grasped some of the key points. In this chapter there are many different ideas on how to do it quickly and effectively giving the teacher ideas for planning their next lesson.

Overview

By now I hope the overview of the Framework is clear and simple to use. So now, read on through the book or go to your area of choice to scan through the ideas you want to try and start designing those outstanding lessons.

USING THE FRAMEWORK TO PLAN

The Framework is designed to allow teachers to plan a lesson before putting it onto the formal lesson planning pro formas. Different versions of the Framework can be used by teachers. Each version has different advantages which are suited to different teachers and different styles.

Version 1:

Outstanding Lesson Framework—Blank Planning Sheet

Firstly, to aid in planning and to help in producing outstanding lessons, a blank form is available next to the Framework itself.

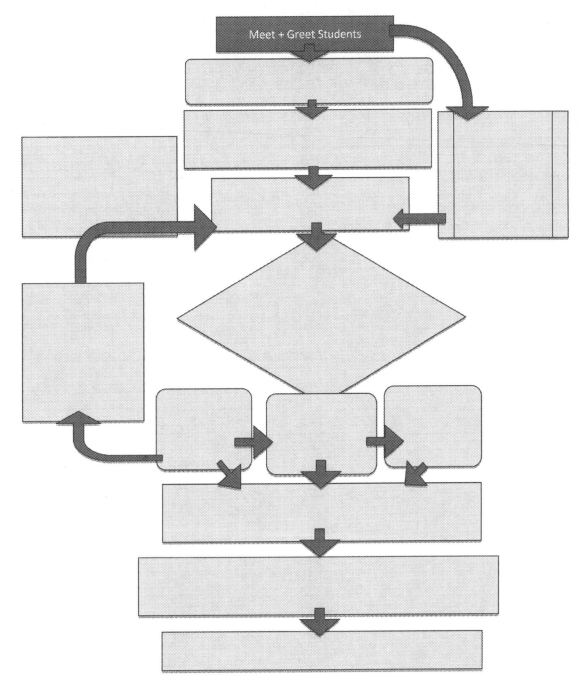

How to Use the Blank

The blank planning sheet can be used to sketch out ideas for the outstanding lesson. Just go to each chapter and choose a technique from each section and fill in the blank form. This will encourage the variety in lessons and can be used in everyday planning. It's simple, easy, and best of all, very quick. Some techniques can be used across different sections. So, be aware a technique in a different chapter can sometimes be used elsewhere. This is only limited by imagination, so be inventive.

This is most apparent in the chapter "Wider Learning Objectives", where there are a selection of techniques that enhance numeracy, literacy, and the use of IT in everyday classes. Have a good look around for inspiration and decide what techniques fit where. At first, applying each chapter is a very good and simple starting place.

Opposite is an example how the Framework has been used by a teacher of a class of five-year-olds on recognising even numbers and working toward halving numbers. The plan for the lesson is panned out in rough ready to be placed on the formal lesson plan pro forma.

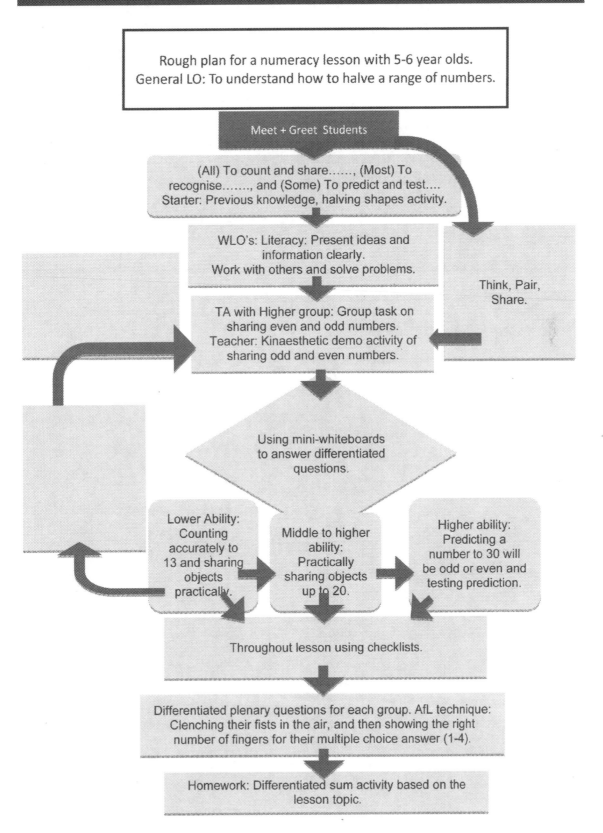

Rough plan for a numeracy lesson with 5-6 year olds.
General LO: To understand how to halve a range of numbers.

Meet + Greet Students

(All) To count and share......, (Most) To recognise......., and (Some) To predict and test.... Starter: Previous knowledge, halving shapes activity.

WLO's: Literacy: Present ideas and information clearly.
Work with others and solve problems.

Think, Pair, Share.

TA with Higher group: Group task on sharing even and odd numbers.
Teacher: Kinaesthetic demo activity of sharing odd and even numbers.

Using mini-whiteboards to answer differentiated questions.

Lower Ability: Counting accurately to 13 and sharing objects practically.

Middle to higher ability: Practically sharing objects up to 20.

Higher ability: Predicting a number to 30 will be odd or even and testing prediction.

Throughout lesson using checklists.

Differentiated plenary questions for each group. AfL technique: Clenching their fists in the air, and then showing the right number of fingers for their multiple choice answer (1-4).

Homework: Differentiated sum activity based on the lesson topic.

Version 2:

Outstanding Lesson Framework and Teaching Ideas

Version 2 allows you to quickly get ideas without going through the chapters. Just go through and decide upon strategies to plan that outstanding lesson. This version is best produced on an A3 size and is available from outstanding lessons made simple in both PDF and laminated form.

Visual, Audio and Kinaesthetic learning styles

A visual learner may respond to:

Diagrams, mind and thinking maps, charts, videos, films, graphs, posters, concept maps, pamphlets, drawing, collages, colour highlighting

An auditory learner may respond to:

Discussion, group work, pair work, debates, interviewing, presentations, improvisations, mnemonics, creating raps or rhymes, using music

A kinaesthetic learner may respond to:

Role-play, drama, model making, card sorts, 'diamond nine' sorting activity, Bend it, three shot showdown and freeze-frames, improvisation

---

The task boxes indicate the main *DIFFERENTIATED* tasks. This should be where the students are "learning by doing" with only guidance from the teacher. Thereby offering the students the chance to **collaborate & be independent** from the teacher. Coupling this work with peer- or self-assessment allows the students to realise their own independent learning skills. It is *essential* for an *outstanding lesson* that this is *majority of the lesson.*

Questions focusing on the learning throughout the lesson
(Use 'think time', 'think/pair/share/square' and 'no hands' rule)

What skills do you have that could be useful this lesson?
What outcomes are you are expecting?
How will you set about learning?
How could you apply what you now know to solve...?
What could be the function of..?
Where could you find evidence for...?
How valid do you think this evidence is...?
What if...?
What does this suggest to you?
Which do you think is more important / significant...?
What conclusions can you draw...?
How did you reach this conclusion?
What have you learned elsewhere that is like this?
How will you apply what you have learnt?
What skills/knowledge have you acquired that you also use elsewhere?

Engaging questioning techniques to assess individual's

AfL Hinge Point Strategies

Use of ....
Mini-whiteboards
Post-it notes
ABCD cards, corners
True/False
Fist and fingers
Circular questioning

Meet and Greet

Display Learning Objectives (LO) + Engaging Starter Activity

Teacher discusses WLO, LO and encourages challenges through differentiated objectives

Teaching period based upon task or skill

Hinge Point Question: Use to decide who to give each task and who to give help.

Do Task A

Do Task B

Do Extension Task

Peer- or self-assessment exercise to allow students to realise where to improve

Plenary: questions on the LO getting progressively harder or metacognitive plenary. Students or teacher communicates what students have learnt and where is the next step.

Reshaping of explanations for those who still don't grasp the key concept

Reshaping of explanations

Teacher communicates next steps either by talking to whole class, groups and individuals using

---

Using Blooms taxonomy to set differentiated LO
Use one of each of the 3 categories of challenge

Low .....1 REMEMBERING ...2 UNDERSTANDING
Medium....3 APPLICATION ....4 ANALYSIS
High.......5 EVALUATION.......6 CREATING

1 REMEMBERING	2 UNDERSTANDING	3 APPLICATION
describe list state	compare explain outline	calculate determine examine
4 ANALYSIS	5 EVALUATION	6 CREATING
analyse distinguish identify	assess evaluate justify	construct design hypothesise

---

Self and Peer Assessment Strategies

Comparison of outcomes against success criteria e.g.

Comment on a comment

Mark schemes/assessment criteria made understandable to learners

Learners reading through and marking their own/each others' work against shared success criteria

Learners reading through and marking their own/each others' work against shared success criteria

The Assessor/Celebrator cards

Two stars and a question

Use of an exemplar students work to model success / objective

Version 3:

Outstanding Lesson Framework Teaching Ideas and the Blank

Teachers have found it useful to have a large A3 version with a blank on the back of the teaching Framework that allows them to be able to see ideas quickly.

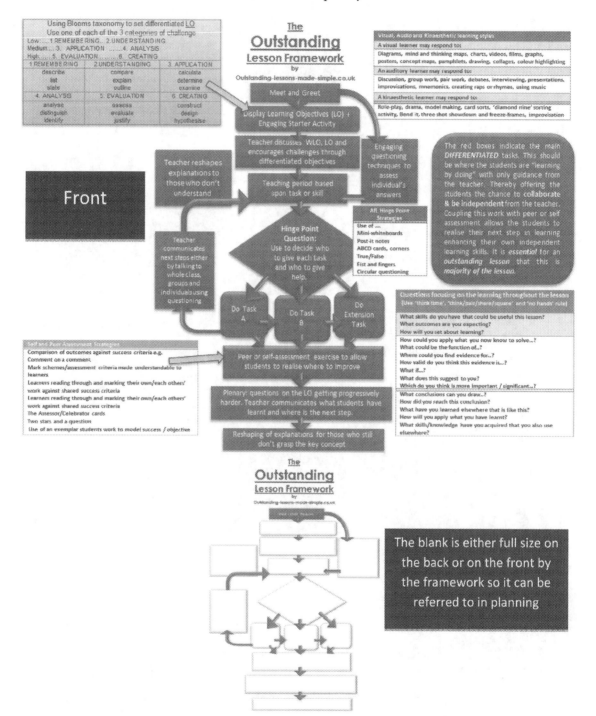

Chapter 1:

MEET AND GREET

Instant Engagement: Saying Hello and Getting to Know

All teachers will know that this section is the most important. If your first ten to fifteen minutes goes wrong, then only an outstanding teacher with an excellent rapport with their class can pull it back. Much like a 100-metre sprint, a winning finish cannot be guaranteed, because some classes are just too difficult to get going with a poor start.

If instant engagement is going to take place, then a routine is always good. Students are comfortable with routines and flourish where there are clear expectations of them with a fair overall approach to both the carrot and the stick.

Let's think about this in terms of the start of the lesson. In younger classes (students with approximate ages between five and ten years), teachers mainly have the same class every day. However, the class comes back in at break/recess and lunch, and who knows what happened and what information can be found out from the kids when they return.

In older classes (students with approximate ages between eleven and eighteen years), different classes are had by teachers every thirty minutes, an hour, or three hours, as is timetabled in some schools. Overall, this means that children are experiencing different stimuli and conversations, and are achieving different goals in their break/recess or lunch, or even at their previous lesson. So, always make it so there is a short time at the start of a lesson to ask one or two of these questions:

- "How are you?"
- "What did you get up to at lunch?"
- "Did you have a good weekend?"
- "Are you ready to learn?"
- "Are you ready for the best lesson ever?"

Remember, this is the chance to get them going and get them in the right mind for learning. Just be aware to make these questions quick, otherwise the start of the lesson and the learning will be delayed. First of all, it will become clear that some students are a bit unsure when faced with a teacher who cares about them outside of their subject/classroom. It may take a few times of asking before they respond. All I say is persevere. How do you know that your students aren't county gymnasts, kickboxing instructors, and world champion chess players? Get used to having these conversations, heap them with praise, and your relationships with the students will flourish. The bonus for learning is, by getting to know the students slightly better, they will want to work harder and achieve more. This all ends in a lesson with great engagement and wonderful atmosphere.

As well as finding out about their accomplishments, it also provides the chance to find out small but important information about them that will help the decision on how to approach them, which is especially important in the morning when you usually haven't seen them for a long time.

All these bits of information help decide what to do or say when the student says these immortal words, "I'm sorry I'm late".

So what's the response? Let's imagine a teacher who talked to this student on a regular basis and knew that they probably had no breakfast; or knew their family never woke them up; or that their parents, frankly, did not care; or even worse, in some cases. Often children of any description don't appreciate being shouted at; but these students are particularly vulnerable as some are not looked after or cared for well. So, many teachers knowing this information, wouldn't launch into a telling off. Often the best response is "Sit down, get started, and we'll speak later".

The child is then immediately engaged in the learning. However, the key point is to never forget to have that conversation afterwards and apply a sanction or offer help should it be necessary.

Are You Prepared?

Preparation is the key moment to everyone's lesson. Are all of the materials prepared and easily accessible to either the teacher or the children? There are some simple tick sheets that can be used when preparing lessons (see below) and fit perfectly with the Framework itself. The most important is the Assessment for Learning (AfL) box. In this box, there is a list of materials that all teachers should have, or that are easily accessible. Keep your AfL box stocked and the lesson will become much easier to assess (without preparation) and to make exciting.

Lesson Prep Tick List	
	Any resources I need are readily accessible to me: Pens ☐ Whiteboard Markers ☐ Interactive Whiteboard Pen if necessary ☐ YouTube or any other Video already downloaded using YouTube video convertor (do not rely on the Internet, many a good lesson has been ruined by Internet connectivity problems) ☐
	Any resources they need are readily accessible to them including: Lined paper ☐ Plain Paper ☐ Graph paper ☐ Coloured Paper Drawers ☐ Pens ☐ Pencils ☐ Crayons ☐ Rulers ☐ Calculators ☐ Glue sticks ☐
	Assessment for Learning Box fully stocked with a mixture of class sets of the following: ABCD Cards ☐ Yes/No cards ☐ True/False cards ☐ Red/Yellow/Green Cards or Cups or Cones ☐ Mini-Whiteboards ☐ Working Whiteboard Pens ☐ Post-its notes ☐ Highlighter pens ☐
	Assessment for Learning Box fully stocked with: A Sponge ball or a Juggling ball ☐ A mock Microphone ☐ Games(e.g. Jenga, Chairs, Don't Panic, Pop-Up Pirate) ☐ Cards with all your students' names on or set of cards with the alphabet on ☐

Once you have your AfL box, make sure you get it restocked every year at the very least. If you are really lucky and your school is always prepared for new ideas, then go to them and ask for an AfL box to be made for each teacher. Cheaper alternatives can be made by asking for the R/Y/G, Y/N, T/F, ABCD, and mini-whiteboards to be included in the student's planners. Many companies will now let you individualise the student's planner and put these cards in there for use at any time.

All teachers need to make Assessment for learning a major focus in outstanding lessons; and the quickest and easiest way is to have a pre-prepared box. It will give you all the resources needed to execute effective assessment without any preparation.

Happy Face

Never ever overtly be unhappy or down when meeting a group, especially for the first time. Children are keen sensors of dislike or boredom from a teacher. If fatigue is there, usually at the start or end of a term, or day, then try to grab some energy from somewhere (usually coffee for a lot of teachers)☺.

If the resources are not top notch because the school can't afford anything else, then don't be negative. This can easily transfer onto the children whose attitudes can develop a lack of enthusiasm for learning over the days, months, and years. An inspirational head once gave a training session for senior leaders and the best advice he gave was for everybody to say a minimum of five positive comments about staff every day. Multiply this ten-fold for students, and it will serve you well.

If Music Be the Food of Love, Play On

This is one of the best things for calming down any errant and excitable students after a break. Play music from a smartphone, tablet, or computer. Luckily most classes have speakers connected to their whiteboard, so it's an easy thing to do. Just make sure it is loud enough to be heard, but not too loud to disturb other classes. If this is built into your routine, then the students will soon ask, "Can I choose the music, Sir?", or, "Where is the music today?"

Straight away without you doing anything but playing a song, the students are engaged with the teacher, and the song can be built into the lesson itself.

There are numerous strategies and here are just a few:

1. **Let music be your starter timer:**
   * Let the students know that the starter must be done by the end of the music.
   * Use a countdown timer on the board if there is access to one, and if not, download one from the Internet and use your projector.

2. **Develop playlists:**
   * Build a list of songs that work.
   * Ditch the songs that don't.
   * Different abilities and ages will work more effectively if the music is tailored toward them so use different music for each group.

3. **Music as a carrot:**
   * Allow the students to choose their song. If they have done well, allow them to choose a song for next lesson from your list.
   * This can also be used for latecomers; if they get to the lesson early, then they can choose the music in the thirty seconds before you let the rest in.

4. Music as a theme of the lesson:

- Introduce the learning objectives for a piece of work to music. This builds a scene and ignites the imagination. For example, when writing a science fiction story, what better music than Gustav Holtz' *The Planets, Mars the Bringer of War*? This has been used in many science fiction/action films, including *Star Wars*, and will set the scene perfectly.
- Perform the introductory sentence like a narrator to background music as intro to a media or ICT lesson. The *Mission Impossible* theme tune is great for this.

5. Use music to allow students to decide on the theme:

- Students can use the music to determine the rough learning objectives.
    - i. A very simple example could be if you are doing a lesson on the periodic table, then use the periodic table song from YouTube.
    - ii. In a literacy lesson, find out how many different films have used this theme music; this again can be done with many classical songs, as many have been used in multiple movies.

6. Different music for different ability groups:

- Of course, different songs work for different groups, so if there is access to tablets, then just get different ability groups around different devices.
- Get any assistants in the lesson involved. Maybe they have a smartphone which they can use. They have a more in-depth knowledge of what works with some students. For example, those with special educational needs (SEN) with whom they are working.

The Summary

Now to get started, remember we are predominantly teaching the kids of twenty-, thirty-and forty-somethings. This means that songs from the students' own era can be used, but it is also good to include songs from different eras, which they will have heard at home. As songs are used with different techniques, think about these prompts:

What is the aim of having the music?

Is it there to wake the students up? Is the aim to make the students lively?

Is it there to get them quiet and focused?

Is the song linked to the lesson?

Are the students working on something else and merely using the song as a timing device?

Most groups will settle down quicker and start to work quicker than usual, and with luck, they will get learning straight away without any prompts.

Chapter 2:
LEARNING OBJECTIVES & STARTERS

Learning Objectives

So why share learning objectives? Does it aid the learning? The answer is yes! If students realise what they are learning and why they are learning it, effort levels are generally raised as well as their enjoyment of the lesson and their self-esteem. By making sure all students know that in their lesson that they have learned something, they will all feel that they are making progress and getting smarter.

Students can only measure their learning and their progress if they know what they are learning today. This can be presented to the students in terms of "We are learning to" (**WALT**) or just given as learning objectives.

The best learning is where students know what they are learning, how they are learning, and in some cases, what is next. This is why observers tend to ask, "What are you learning today?"

Therefore, the writing and sharing of learning objectives is vitally important to deliver outstanding learning which will be discussed throughout this chapter. Other questions are often asked by observers, one of which includes, "How do you know you got [grade or level] . . . . ?"

This is where success criteria come into play. A success criterion allows a student to recognise that they have achieved. They should always be clearly linked to each learning objective. The important part is that they do not give away the answer. They must only give a structure, where the student can recognise that they are on the right lines and achieving. This is commonly presented as "What I am looking for" (**WILF**), or put simply, as success criteria.

So, let's see an example in literacy.

Personification—The Act of Humanising an Object

The students need to know what the meaning of personification. They are then meant to use it to create a poem that embodies this skill. So, here is an example of a simple learning objective with its accompanying success criteria:

Learning Objective: We are learning to (**WALT**) recognise personification in a poem.

Success Criteria: What I am looking for (**WILF**) is that I have used personification three times in my poem in different situations.

This means the students can now recognise that they have been successful through the objectives being made explicit within the success criteria. Outstanding lessons often have simple success criteria linked to each learning objective, so all the students can access the learning and feel they have achieved.

There will be more details on learning objectives and their links to success criteria in the form of self-and peer-assessment mentioned later on in the book; but for now, let's consider making learning objectives fun and engaging.

The first simple rules with learning objectives are:

1. Display them where all students can easily see.
2. Make sure they are clear from the start of the lesson.
3. If possible, make sure they are visible all the way through the lesson.

Quick tip

It is easy to achieve all these things with the right tools. So, put in a request to your head teacher/head of department for a small whiteboard to be placed on your wall. This will be just for learning objectives or success criteria, which are placed up during the entire lesson.

Writing Learning Objectives

There are many effective ways to write a learning objective, but the whole aim here is to keep it simple. So there are a few guidelines to get started, which are designed to be helpful as possible to keep you learning objectives:

Here it is broken down a little further:

Specific   Is the learning objective defined and easy to understand and follow?
Measurable   Can it be assessed during the lesson?
Achievable   Can it be achieved in the time given?
Relevant   Is it relevant to your course, the learning, and wider key skills?
Time Related Are there rough timings for each objective?

If you keep this in mind when writing objectives, you won't go wrong. The next step is to actually start writing them, and this is where differentiation comes into play.

Differentiation is where teachers provide different pathways for students to learn in ways so that they can all achieve. This can be accomplished in different ways:

1. Where some students arrive at different end-points
2. Where the students all reach the same learning through different pathways provided by the teacher
3. Where the teacher assigns different roles and responsibilities that require different amounts of skill

In any outstanding lesson, differentiation is a necessity because it means all students can learn regardless of ability.

In order to plan differentiated approaches, it is necessary to write learning objectives which have different levels of challenge. These are called differentiated learning objectives. The first step is to focus on the golden rules:

> ## Must be learning-related and based upon a skill not an outcome

> ## Write using the new Bloom's Taxonomy

New Bloom's Taxonomy

Bloom's Taxonomy is a collection of verbs of increasing difficulty, which can be used to construct a learning objective. It is shown underneath in the order of difficulty, lowest to highest.

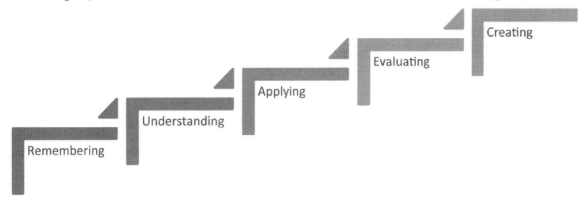

Classified underneath each title are a multitude of verbs which can be used to write different learning objectives. They can then be used for delivering challenge in lessons through the Framework. For easy access, a small selection of the different verbs is displayed with the Framework so objectives can be created easily and quickly. The verbs in the table below are in Framework Version 2 and are some of the most commonly used in lessons. Therefore, they are a great start to writing good objectives and delivering the right level of challenge in lessons.

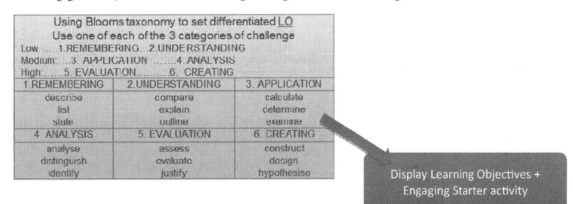

Most lessons contain three different levels of challenge by picking verbs from three different areas of Bloom's Taxonomy. For example, remembering, understanding and application sections allow the creation of three different expectations for students and is commonly known as differentiated Learning Objectives (LO). The LOs rise in challenge as the students progress through them, and are commonly presented in the following format:

All students should be able to . . .
Most students should be able to . . .
Some students should be able to . . .

The learning objectives writing process is just to choose the level of pitch in the lesson and pick the most appropriate verbs. Here are some examples:

Science

- ALL students should *determine* independent and dependent variables.
- MOST students should *identify* control variables.
- SOME should design & *justify* a fair test.

English

- ALL must be able to *identify* persuasive techniques.
- MOST should be able to *analyse* their effects.
- SOME could apply persuasive techniques to *construct* a speech.

This book is about making things as simple as possible, so what is better than to have all of the verbs in one place for ease? For this aim, just look at the great resources all readily available on the Internet. Search "Bloom's Taxonomy" and look at the images produced. One that is thoroughly recommended is the diagram on the next page, although there are many others.

The difficulty gets higher as you go darker on the diagram, going from remembering to creating.

- **Level 1**(inner circle) is "Remember" to "Create" sections.
- **Level 2** then delivers a wider variety of verbs for all of the key processes.
- **Level 3** gives ideas about possible resources and learning tasks that arise from the use of the verbs.
- **Level 4** gives information on personal learning and thinking skills which will be discussed later on in the book. This resource not only facilitates the writing of learning objectives but also gives ideas on how to get the students to learn as well.

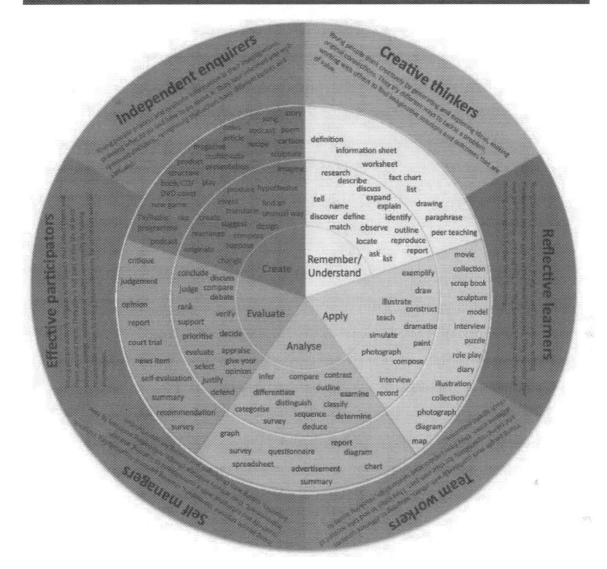

Bloom's Taxonomy with Personal Learning and Thinking Skills

Learning Objectives Teaching Ideas

How Are They Going to Learn Today?

In lessons, each learning objective is usually accompanied by a task like a science practical, a form of physical activity, a play, extended writing or even a role play. This technique involves the teacher communicating what the students are going to do and how they are going to do it as soon as they enter. This can make students feel safe and confident whilst igniting their interest immediately. It is particularly effective for students with Special Educational Needs (SEN) and helps you develop a routine of planning where students can immediately know what they are doing.

Quick tip

Use a Velcro board with different cards with animations on and place them up before every lesson so the children understand. This does involve a little bit of resource-making, but it also delivers a lot of benefit in the long run. Just decide on the main activities that happen in your lessons and make a set of cards with animations for them, get a bit of Velcro and quickly attach them at the start of the lesson.

Disappearing Learning Objectives

We all want students to realise what they are learning and what better way to do it than to set them with a challenge.

Put the learning objectives up for a time limit—say, thirty seconds—and then make them disappear. This can be done easily by using PowerPoint animation timings. Stop the lesson at any point and ask, "What are we meant to be learning today?"

Anagrammed Learning Objectives

Take the learning objectives and turn them into anagrams. The difficulty can be set according to the students, so easily differentiated. They just need to be engaging and inform the students clearly what they are learning. Some examples of learning objectives are given underneath with the anagrams at the end.

Can you work out the anagram? The answers are in the footnote at the bottom of the page.

We are learning to describe a setting using **reuse sons.**

We are learning to multiply using a **columned moth**.

Quick
tip

Wordsmith is a website which can create anagrams from keywords entered. You can also visit wordsmith.org/anagram/animation.html which can create an image of the learning objectives being rearranged. This can be used to give the students the answer, which is smart and very visual.

Jumbled Up Learning Objectives

A simpler, easier version related to anagrams would be to just jumble the words in the learning objectives:

We multiply learning column use are to the method.

This can be made harder or easier by combining techniques. Jumble up the objectives for your lower-ability students and use the Wordsmith website to anagram for your higher-ability students. They should finish at very similar times discussing and comparing their answers to each other.

Answers We are learning to describe a setting using **our senses**.
We are learning to multiply using a column method.

Pictionary Learning Objectives

Pictionary can be used in many ways in a lesson. Here are some suggestions with learning objectives:

1. Take one of the keywords from the objective and get a student to draw an image based on the keyword; then get the class to guess what they are describing.
2. Create a drawing describing the learning and let the children figure it out.

Students Find Out What the Learning Objectives Are

Don't tell them what the objectives are. At some point during the lesson, they will have to make up the learning objectives. It can even be used as a sum up to the lesson (plenary). Just ask, "What would your learning objectives be now that you've had your lesson?"

This can also be done using Post-it notes, which can be placed on the board. All the students write their learning objective on the Post-it note. Get them to write what they feel they learned today and maybe give them a selection of verbs to use from Bloom's Taxonomy. This means they can be quickly assessed or better still get them to assess each other and begin a discussion.

The Greeter:

All Visitors Are Welcome

This is a fantastic tool and an engaging way to develop students' confidence. It is also a positive role where the student is given responsibility as well as a forum to practice their listening and speaking skills.

The Greeter is a simple card (below right) that is given to the students, which instructs them to meet and greet anyone who comes into the classroom. The cards go onto describe to the observer, or anyone who enters, what the class is learning today.

Some guidelines for using the Greeter are suggested below, however, it does depend on the class:

Instructions for the student:

- Stand up and say hello first.
- Only meet and greet if I (the teacher) nod.
- Describe the learning objective you are doing at this time.
- Be confident and stand tall. The person you're speaking to will be much more taken aback than you.

This is a fantastic way for the students to be unpredictable and encouraging and to own their own learning. It also keeps the children just that little bit on edge and focused, both listening intently to the teacher and ready to pounce on any person who ventures through the door.

Quick tip

Keep a set of these differentiation role cards in your pocket for ideas at any time without preparation. The full set is described throughout the book. If you would like a full set, visit outstanding-lessons-made-simple.co.uk/shop.

Starter Activities

The aim of a starter activity is purely to get the learning started by getting the students in the right frame of mind. It can be based on the subject or just on getting the brain warmed up and ready for action (a hook).

It is possible to start the learning within seconds of the students opening the door. To achieve this though, again there are some simple questions to ask.

Is the starter accessible?

Is it engaging? Does it grab the student's attention?

Is it related to the style or content of the learning in the lesson?

Is it related to time?

If the answer is "yes" to these questions, it is a great starter. The best way to develop this skill is to have a starter in every single lesson so they are used to it and ready to fly.

Quick tip

Ideas should always be used in combination with each other to make an imaginative and engaging lesson. For example, combine music and a learning objective starter like Pictionary. This gets the students used to a timed starter to music. The students must complete the starter by the end of the music. Students will get engaged quickly, and the learning environment is far simpler and easier.

Sum Activity

This is an easily differentiated activity that provides challenging problems that students love regardless of ability. The process is as follows:

- Write a simple question.
- The answer begins the next question.
- This means the students only progress through the questions if they can answer the previous question correctly.
- All the questions are on prior learning.
- The final answer relates to the lesson.
- It can go on for as many levels as the teacher wishes or has time.

This is great for problem solving because when the students have the final answer, it can be a clue to a question and not actually the final answer. The answer may be, for example:

- The identity of a thing/person/feeling/a chemical, etc.
- A role of a person or an object (e.g. job or design of box)
- A process, such as addition, multiplication, or hiring a person

Children are often dying to know the answer in all kinds of abilities and behaviourally challenging groups. It can be done in any lesson but probably easiest in numerical subjects.

An example is below, which was used in a maths lesson for twelve-year-olds; it builds on prior learning using mental maths (no calculators). The answer is guiding the student to the main subject of the lesson, shapes. Can you do it? Check the answer in the footnote.[2]

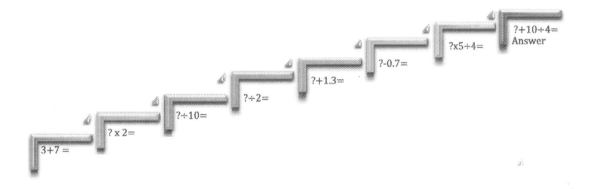

Calculate the answer, what shape has that number of sides?

Scrabble

In any lesson, we can use a simple adaptation of Scrabble where each letter has a number indicating its value (e.g. "Z" is ten and "E" is one).

Give the students a list of letters (randomly or not), just like Scrabble. If it is not random, then try designing it so that the letters are the right ones to make a selection of keywords to be used in the lesson. The students' aim is then to generate the largest points from their letters.

---

[2]   The answer is 3, so the shape is triangle

This is easily differentiated by doing one or all of these:

- Giving some students more difficult letters (e.g. more higher numbered letters)
- Giving them a number of letters or a total to aim towards
- Restricting their starting letter

For example, tell one student to get at least a five-letter word and another to get at least a six-letter word. Remember, you make up the letters.

For producing random letters, try a random letter generator such as www. randomlettergenerator.com. For ease in lessons, buy Scrabble or another letter game for your AfL box so letters can be pulled out of a bag; this also means scores can be counted up. This also allows a bit of competition which can develop engagement, pace, and children's willingness to participate in challenging activities.

Number Generators

Just as letters can be generated with Scrabble, why not have starters with number generators like the game show *Countdown*? Number generators can be used to get students to create a number through different methods (e.g. subtraction, addition, multiplication, and division). This can be differentiated using different target numbers and different methods (e.g. only use + and/or - and/ or ÷ and/or x).

A free and easy *Countdown*-style game can be found on the Internet at www. purely-games.com/countdown.html. There is also a *Countdown* app for tablets or smartphones.

Boggle

This is yet another classic game that can be used for learning, much like Scrabble, but now it's going to be a competition for the largest amount of words that can be generated in say, three minutes. Remember, if it is all about keywords, then make the created words be related to the subject of the lesson.

Consider a physical education lesson about different muscles; jot down nine letters that can include the keywords of the lesson (e.g. tricep or bicep) and get them to play. This is good fun and a great game to get students engaged.

There are loads of web-based games like this; however, for one that is simple and easy to use, try www.wordplays.com/boggle.

Question Relay

This engaging starter is extremely competitive and immediate. Simply print and prepare, say, five questions, which can be linked to the levels of differing challenge in the class.

Quick tip

Setting up challenge: Follow Bloom's Taxonomy when creating the questions so they are getting tougher as they progress. If there is added indication of progress and differentiation, they can be linked to levels or grades.

Next step is to split the students into teams of four as they walk in. Get one student from each team to come up and get the first question (the least challenging) from the teacher. They take this back to their group, and all agree on an answer.

A different student from the group takes it back to the teacher who either gives them question two or gives them a clue to aid in answering question one to take back to their group. Repeat this process either until the timer runs out or one team wins by reaching and answering question five. Give out heaps of praise if they reach five, I have even heard one teacher saying to the class before they started, "No one has ever reached five. Be the first."

It set out the stall and everyone lapped up the challenge in a middle-ability group.

Here is an example of a question relay used in a citizenship lesson in a mixed-ability group. Students were fully engaged in politics and society, an impressive achievement by the teacher concerned.

1. What is the capital of the UK? Who is the Prime Minister? (Grade D)
2. Describe what a democracy is. (Grade C)
3. Explain how communism is different to democracy. (Grade B)
4. Evaluate the impact of the coalition of government. (Grade A)

Mystery Box

Find a box and just put some question marks on it and call it the "mystery box". This starter is all about the curiosity of the students and their desire to find out what the mystery is!

Think of a lesson topic to introduce or a previous topic to assess. Now find some objects that are either closely related and/or loosely linked to the topic. Place a mixture of the objects into the box.

Now get the students to take one item at a time out of the mystery box and ask them to describe what the box contents mean or show.

Take an example of a geography lesson, either introducing or assessing the knowledge of the water cycle with the box's contents, including:

- Cotton wool
- Bottle of water
- A rock
- Cocktail stick umbrella

The students were asked to take one out at a time, linking the objects to topic. They were then asked to feedback to the teacher using mini-whiteboards.

Quick tip

This idea is easy to differentiate and to place the emphasis on the students. To differentiate, just make different boxes for different abilities. Higher-abilities students can have looser links to the topic where their thought processes have to be more open ended. Also, with three to four different boxes, each table may have a slightly different experience.

So use a mystery box and excite the students, and vary it as much as you like. Get them to feel, get them to hear, or see, or a combination of all.

Find the Fib

Just write a series of sentences and make sure one of them is a mistruth or a lie. Students must spot which one. For example, can you find the lie below?

A. Global warming is where the earth has warmed due to the excess release of carbon dioxide by the burning of all fuels.
B. Global warming is where the temperature has increased resulting in higher global temperatures.

This is a simple example where A is incorrect (not all fuels produce carbon dioxide), and B is correct. A further challenge would be to make students justify their answer. It can be made very difficult to spot the incorrect one, so, it's all about how difficult you want to make it.

Google Translator

This is a great way of getting students to recognise and remember keywords that are important in a topic or piece of work. It also allows the combination of subjects to stretch the students.

Write a sentence and then translate it using Google Translator (or any other translator) into another language like French or Spanish. Make sure to use the keywords that are similar in the language used so the students can recognise them and try to construct the sentence. For example, in maths introducing a lesson on triangles:

On the whiteboard write: "Cette forme est un **triangle** et un **triangle** a **trois** côtés."

In this sentence, the easier words to recognise are in **bold**. Then just get the students to construct the sentence. The answer is: This shape is a triangle, and a triangle has three sides.

Quick tip

To differentiate, put up numerous different sentences making each a little more complex usually by adding more detail. Students then choose which one to translate. Remember this is not a language lesson; the words must be close to English but not quite the same.

Five Ws

This can be used in any area of the lesson or as part of a starter. This technique is very open ended depending on the subject. Place the topic or question of the lesson on the board and ask the students to create questions based upon the Fives Ws:

Who? What? When? Where? Why?

This can even be used in conjunction with the Find a Fib starter:

- Why is A wrong?
- Why is B right?
- What can you do to B to make it more detailed?
- Why does carbon dioxide increase global temperatures?
- Where is the temperature increasing the most and why?
- Who is contributing towards this increase?
- What is it?
- When did it start?
- What location will be the most effected?
- Why is it happening most now?

Find the Most Correct Statement

This is slight adaptation on Find the Fib; just find the one statement which is the most correct. This is an altogether more challenging task. It can be very open depending on how it is presented; and will often look simple to the students, however, it can be incredibly difficult depending on its design. An example of a simple version is shown below:

Option A: A full stop stops a sentence.

Option B: A sentence with a capital letter is stopped by a full stop. ✓

In an outstanding lesson, challenging work, and overt differentiation is an expectation from the beginning. This certainly isn't challenging and takes the student five seconds to accomplish. So consider this: design "Find the Most Correct Statement" with only a lack of a small detail. Take a look at this:

Revised Option A: A full stop ends a sentence where a sentence is begun with a capital letter.

Revised Option B: A full stop ends a sentence, where all commas, capital letters, and colons are used correctly.

Revised Option C: A full stop ends a sentence where a sentence begins with a capital letter and, if needed, has a comma separating phrases.

All are correct, but which is most correct? This is a fairly open task and can lead to a class discussion and development of success criteria if you wish to take it that far.

The higher-ability students will give more detailed responses, however the lower-ability students will still recognise the important information and be part of the discussion.

Snowball Fight

Snowball is an excellent way of beginning a discussion on a subject in an exciting way. It is not for the faint-hearted though, because it can look like chaos; buts it well worth trying.

Think of a task where you need to generate ideas or compare and contrast students' answers. Get the students to write their ideas or answers onto a piece of plain paper. The paper is then scrunched up into a "snowball." The "snowball" is then thrown by the students at anyone in the classroom (optionally, to include the teacher) once and once only. This may mean that thirty are thrown each time. The teacher calls "stop" and instructs each person to pick up one "snowball" and read the answers or ideas on the paper.

Students can then be told to add or amend ideas and the "snowballs" can then be scrunched up and thrown again. This is repeated as many times as you need to generate ideas or get the correct answers. It can also be done in pairs or groups and used as a good, exciting start to any lesson.

Quick tip

Alternatively, if snowballs aren't suitable for the class, then get the students to make paper aeroplanes and transport the ideas this way. It's a little less harsh. Let your imagination be your guide on this, or better still, ask the children what they want to make.

Keyword Finder

A classic and brilliant way of increasing literacy in your subject, in fact, every subject, involves many keywords, which are integral to learning. It is the teacher's role to focus on keywords as much as possible in the context of the lesson.

The simple approach is to find as many keywords as possible from a media (e.g. a video, a piece of writing, or an audio recording).

If time is available, it is worth making the resources, and if there is administrative support (rare, but it does happen), then do this:

1) Print the keywords on cardboard and get them laminated.
2). Apply Velcro to the back.
3). Get an old piece of chipboard from the technology or maintenance department, or old backing board, then purchase some felt to cover it.

Place the keywords on the new board ready for the lesson. This can even be done as the students say the keywords throughout the lesson. Even better, every time a keyword is said; ring a bell, or give out a prize—think of it like a game show such as *QI*.

Quick tip

Alternatively, if time or money is limited, then use a whiteboard as your keyword board. This means the words are permanently displayed throughout the lesson with all the keywords to discuss.

Thunks

Thunks are unanswerable questions which are accessible to all students no matter what their ability is. Everybody's opinion is valid, which makes them ideal for engaging starters. Be careful though, as they can easily go on for too long if the discussion is side-tracked.

Let's consider a lesson on the nature of sound or hearing. We want to get the students discussing sound or hearing, so how about this for a starter thunk: "If a house falls down, and no one is around, does it make a sound?"

As teachers, we can begin the discussion by tailoring it toward the nature of sound as waves, and the nature of hearing as a detector of waves. This is easily done and everybody can engage in it—so go ahead—do a thunk.

Quick tip

There is also a book available called *The Little Book of Thunks* and a very useful web-site, www.thunks.co.uk, where you can find all manner of useful thunks to get your lesson started.

Convert This into a Picture

Write a key idea on the board to start the lesson, then get the students to convert the idea into a picture or a series of pictures. Students are converting information and, therefore, learning through doing. Furthermore, it is a great way to initiate memory and to get the students to understand what they are doing. For example:

"Think of a history lesson for 8-9 year olds on invaders and settlers. Timeline—Vikings invade Lindesfarne. First wave is in AD 798. How can you portray that in one single image? You have three minutes."

Take a look at the example done using a tablet by an eight-year-old pupil. Imagine again combining techniques. What if the "Five Ws" were now used in relation to the picture? There are many more questions that could arise and help develop the theme of the lesson.

Develop a Question

This is a running theme throughout this book: outstanding lessons involve students who always question and want to further their learning. They don't always automatically have this trait, so it needs to be nurtured.

So, why not give them some information and make them all ask two to three questions on that subject. For more structure, use the "Five Ws". Use the feedback from the class to start off the lesson and introduce the new and interesting lesson topic.

Entrance Ticket

This is where questions are asked on the lesson topic as soon as the students enter the room. This means they are immediately engaged. The students are posed a question, usually on the board as they enter, and given Post-it, or sticky, notes on which to write their answers. The note is then placed in the teacher's hand so they can take a quick glance, or they are brought up and stuck onto the whiteboard. It is a good idea to get them to write their initials/name on the note to identify who gave what answer. The Post-it notes can be read out as they are handed in, or you can get the students to place them on the board. This can prompt a discussion on their answers and develop a hook for the lesson topic depending on your aims.

Summary on Starters and Learning Objectives

Listed throughout this chapter are clear starter activities, including those involving learning objectives. Each example is designed to include clear guidance on how to use them, often offering ideas on differentiating, or websites that would be helpful all through our quick tips. However, it's useful to summarise the main points:

- It's good to make starters relate to the previous lesson although this is not essential.
- Starters can be used to introduce a new topic using common knowledge.
- Use simple games where appropriate and where they work in terms of learning.
- Give structure to questioning using techniques such as the "Five Ws".
- Try to use something that ignites the imagination to get the students interested (the hook).
- Learning objectives can be engaging and not just boring, so be imaginative.
- The Internet has loads of word games, number games, and puzzles, so use them.
- Where possible, differentiate the starter. This is recommended especially in mixed-ability classes in both secondary and primary.
- Lastly, bear in mind any technique in this book can be adapted as a starter, especially those in the next section.

Chapter 3:
CHALLENGE AND WIDER LEARNING OBJECTIVES

Introducing and Developing Challenge

"Kites rise highest against the wind, not with it." (Winston Churchill)

First of all, developing challenges is essential to an outstanding lesson! It has to be celebrated with abundant enthusiasm to get it embedded. Challenge has to be regular and well planned with effective help in place to guide the students through if needed.

Challenging activities are designed in such a way that all students feel that the learning is achievable and challenging. This is one of the most difficult tasks for a teacher to design, so let's consider the starting point and a few simple tips:

- Be positive about the challenge in the room.
- Make sure everyone knows it's achievable.
- Describe the differentiated learning objectives using Bloom's Taxonomy where appropriate.
- Remind the students regularly of their successes, from meet and greet to plenary.

Wider Learning Objectives

This is a key focus where all teachers have to be teachers of literacy and numeracy throughout all ages of education. Whole-school focus on literacy and numeracy will inevitably increase results across the board. So, how do we thread literacy, numeracy, and other wider skills such as information communication technology (ICT) throughout the lesson?

What is majorly important is that all the wider skills are adding to the learning. Let's take the example of using ICT in the form of Excel in your lesson. If students are writing a list of characteristics out about, say, a poem or story, do they need to use Word or Excel to do it?

Depending on what age you are teaching, is it really a skill to type this using Word? This, of course, depends on the age and ability levels of the students. Be aware if the students have practiced this skill a hundred times and have done so utilising Word or Excel because this will just serve to waste time in the lesson and does not really add anything new.

To ensure that ICT adds to the learning, just make sure that it introduces something new. For example, choose some different macros or applications within the piece of software that the students must use. In the case of a poem, maybe look for the correct use of styles like italics for quotes, the use of different fonts, colours, and font sizes to emphasis keywords, phrases and emotion. This adds to the activity and uses ICT skills that will benefit the student in all subjects. In this way, students can learn a subject through ICT whilst acquiring a new ICT skill.

Quick tip This can be done in many other ways in Microsoft Office and only the teacher's IT knowledge is the limit. So if you're not sure, ask a friendly ICT technician or teacher for advice because I'm sure they can help beef up ICT in a lesson.

Let's now go through different types of wider learning objectives and how they can be incorporated into a lesson.

Literacy

Not everybody is an English teacher or literacy specialist, so it is helpful to know that literacy is not as beguiling as it first may seem. This is by no means a literacy book, but here are some simple approaches to looking at literacy in other subjects:

- **Keywords**—What keywords am I using in my subject? Are they new?
- **Writing Skills**—Spelling, punctuation, and grammar (SPAG); types of descriptive sentences (e.g. simple, compound, or complex); report writing styles; magazine articles.
- **Oral Skills**
  - What are they discussing? Are they reflecting on their work? Are they discussing new ideas?
  - What are they presenting? Are they presenting their work in any way, shape, or form?

Keywords

As already mentioned, it is important in any subject that the keywords are overt (see "Keyword Finder"). For an outstanding lesson, the communication and display of keywords can often be the starting focus.

So here are some starting ideas for teaching using keywords:

Glossary

Students can create their subject keyword glossary. They simply need to identify a place which they can access anytime, such as the back of their exercise book, or a separate little book. In lessons when a keyword is mentioned, students jot it down and describe it in their glossary. This can be used in the future when discussing activities where the keywords are used.

Quick tip

Get them thinking by writing the keyword with its correct spelling in the first lesson and then teach the lesson incorporating the word. In the second lesson, ask them to define it in their glossary. By leaving gaps between when the word was introduced and when the student was asked to define it, it can help students learn and recall the meaning.

Keyword Finder

This is a Velcro board with laminated words or a section of your own whiteboard devoted to the keywords of the lesson or topic.

Writing Frames

Give the students a start to their sentences or a structure for their discussion. This is all about clear prompts to initiate learning; however, it is essential that it is pitched so that the students are doing the majority of the work. The frame is there to give them a start and, therefore, the confidence to attempt and complete the work.

Crosswords

Try writing crosswords based upon the keywords. Depending on how hard you make it, it can really make the students think. Why not get the students to create their own based upon keywords from your topic? This makes the students think hard when asking and answering the questions.

Quick tip

When the students are creating the crossword, differentiate by giving students different keywords according to their ability.
If a crossword is being given to the class to complete, then give two crosswords to your class of varying difficulty.
The Discovery Channel has a simple crossword builder which can be used by both teachers and students. It creates a crossword simply, while at the same time, looking really professional.
Try puzzlemaker.discoveryeducation.com/CrissCrossSetupForm.asp.

Reverse Gap Fills

Give the students a selection of keywords and then ask them a question, or pose a problem. Students then answer by using the keywords and constructing a sentence or paragraph.

Quick tip

To differentiate, set students targets, such as three or four specific keywords as a minimum. It is best to create the questions so that the more keywords they use in their answer, the higher the level they achieve.

Starts with a . . .

Choosing a topic, get the students to name as many keywords that begin with a specific letter in a specific time frame.

Word Splat

Place a set of keywords/numbers/phrases on the board. Get the students to write questions for those keywords/numbers/phrases. Choose two people from the class and bring them up to the board. Randomly choose students to ask their questions, and students at the board can splat the answer when they hear the question. This is great fun and is also competitive, so it gets the children interested from the off. You can make it even more fun by buying a fly swatter, or a rubber mallet to do the job, or keep it simple and just use their hands.

Concept Maps

This is a diagram showing the relationships between concepts and is similar to a mind map. It can be used as a revision tool or a homework and is used to consolidate learning or as a differentiated task in a lesson. As it is completely student led, it is a great tool for developing independence. Here is how it could work:

- Keywords are chosen by the student or given to the student on a topic.
- Concepts (keywords) are usually placed in boxes or circles.
- The keywords are connected with labelled arrows in any direction by the student, and he or she decides how to organise them.
- The relationship between the keywords can usually be expressed using linking phrases and/or verbs such as "due to", "results in", "is required by", or "contributes to".
- The arrow indicates the direction in which you read.

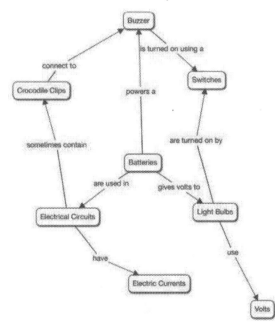

Above is an example of a concept map by an eleven-year-old student, who used the free app called Mental. Can you spot any misconceptions or mistakes? Concept maps are great for spotting misconceptions and allowing the teacher to address them.

Quick tip

If the school is lucky enough to have class sets of tablets, then use Mental by Jean-Yves Vocisano. It is a fantastic resource for creating concept maps and is highly engaging. Maps can be created easily and exported as a PDF. This can be uploaded onto the VLE and displayed on the whiteboard for all the students to analyse and evaluate.

Word Loops

These are a set of questions which are produced with keywords as the answers. Here are the steps:

- Prepare a table with two columns and as many rows as required to have one question per row (usually one question per student in the class).
- Place the questions in column one.
- Next jumble up the answers and place them in column two; it is important the question does not match the answer next to it in column one.
- Use a guillotine to cut out each row; so, for example, there are thirty rows, each with a question and an answer on it.
- Give each student a row (a question and an answer).
- A student starts by reading out loud his or her question, and then waits for someone with the right answer to reply.
- Once the right answer is called out by another student, the student who read out the correct answer reads out his or her question until the whole class has read their questions and answers.
- To make it interesting, you can set this as a challenge. Can the class do it in, say, two minutes? Or, perhaps you could set up a class competition board so that they can beat their friends.

Quick tip

To do this easily, write out your questions in a table created in Word. Then write the answers one row down. Repeat until you have enough questions and answers. The last question's answer is placed in the top box. Then cut up each row and hand each individual slip out. Keep in a plastic bag for future use. To differentiate, make each question more difficult as you go along. Then give the harder questions to the more able students. A very simple example is shown below:

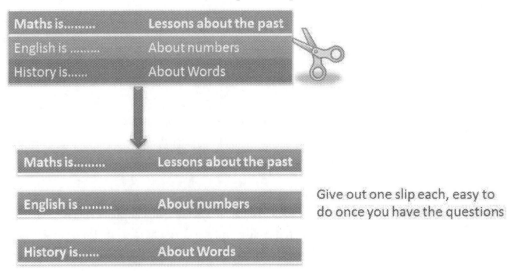

78

Linking Games

Six Degrees of Separation

It is said that everybody in the world can be linked by six degrees of separation. So why not turn it into a class task. For example, "How can Mahatma Ghandi and Winston Churchill be linked through six or less degrees of separation?"

This can be used to consolidate on a topic or start a new one. The answers will be fun and varied and create a buzz in the room.

Tedious Link

This refers to a very similar concept to six degrees of separation but not just linked to people. This is a development of an old radio show feature with a DJ called Comedy Dave. He played one song, explaining how the song was linked to the last show's feature song. It would be a deliberately ramshackle and vague succession of linking "facts", some real and some ludicrous. After the song, any of the real facts contested by the team or listeners were debated, giving Dave the chance to explain and defend his logic. When done with students, the tedious link can be anything as long as the class can defend their choices afterwards. This is an excellent reflective task where there are essentially no wrong answers allowing everybody to be involved no matter their ability.

Quick tip
To differentiate, just limit how many levels are created or give different groups different degrees of separation. Both linking games are very good starting or reviewing activities and lots of fun. They also tick the differentiation, challenge, engagement and cross-curricular boxes.

Key Writing Skills

By giving students a writing frame through which to present their work, it can also give relevance in everyday life. For example, writing up a mathematical relationship can be done in the style of an exam question, or a model answer, which is all very formal. However, once the imagination flows, it can be done as a newsflash about a recent discovery or a diary entry or a magazine article in a journal. There are a myriad of ideas; however, the best bit of advice would be to go and see an English teacher. By doing this, they may be able to help design tasks and develop cross-curricular links.

There are some simple rules that all subjects can adopt to help with writing and they range from the simple to very hard. However, we will only concentrate on the simple stuff because all teachers are not English teachers but all teach literacy as part of their lesson.

The tips are:

- Have an agreed way, usually set down by your school, of marking SPAG in all subjects.
- Encourage the use of point, evidence, and explain (PEE). In English teacher language, this refers to simple, compound, and complex sentences. These structure justifications and evaluations as well as focus the students writing.
- Most students (usually from the age of eight onward at the latest) will recognise simple, compound, and complex or point, evidence, and explain when they are writing in your subject.
- Here is an example of how it helps when justifying an opinion in maths:

Simple (Point)	This shape is a triangle.
Compound (Evidence)	This shape is a triangle and a triangle has three sides.
Complex (Explain)	This shape is a triangle because it has three sides, despite the fact that the sides are different lengths.

Talking and Presenting Your Work

Literacy in lessons can be shown just using normal teaching methods, especially when referring to talking and presenting work. The focus throughout an outstanding lesson is on independence and collaboration. This means it is recommended that lessons regularly include discussion-based work.

This is a key aspect of literacy where students discuss ideas, collaborate, and reflect on the ideas they have produced. Here are some simple ways to get the students talking; however, with all of them, strict timings are necessary as discussed earlier in the "Pace" section under "Key Themes of the Outstanding Lesson Framework".

So here we go with the tips and ideas:

Think-Pair-Square-Share

Discuss a topic, and then give students two minutes to come up with answers/explanations/suggestions surrounding this topic. Then, pair them up to discuss the answers. The pairs then form up to create a square (group of four) and all ideas are shared and discussed. The designated leader, or whomever the teacher picks, feeds back to the teacher after the discussion period.

Word Association Games

This is just like Mallet's Mallet. Purchase a sponge or blow-up mallet from any toy shop. Then, get students to say words that are linked together by association. Start with a keyword related to the subject of the lesson and see where it goes. If they repeat, hesitate, or fail to answer; tap them gently on their head with the sponge/blow-up mallet. If this is uncomfortable, don't do it. This is just a way of making the lesson more fun. It's a great way of getting students engaged and discussing their answers.

This discussion can be promoted by just asking "Why?" A simple connection can be made and guided by the teacher to begin the lesson. I have seen a teacher going round with the mallet doing simple word association games as the students were working. This is genius and lots of fun. The following is a short transcript of a teacher's discussion. It shows that from a short game beginning the discussion, a much more complex process can come into play by just using "Why?"

Question: "Why did Emma think Green was linked to roots? Roots are not green."

Answer: "Roots are a part of plants, Miss."

Question: "Alright then, what plants have to do with green?"

Answer: "Plants are green."

Question: "Why?"

Quick tip Differentiate by changing the starting keyword. More able students may use more obscure and difficult keywords.

The Scribe

Split the groups into three, appointing one student to be the scribe. The other team members are taught something, or shown an image by the teacher, independent of the scribe. During this time the scribe's eyes must be closed.

The scribe then interprets everything they are told by their fellow team members and produces an interpretation through a drawing. This works particularly well if there is a picture, because there is no teaching or talking necessary. To make this more fun, introduce a bit of competition between groups to see who interprets the information quickly and most accurately. The teacher can walk around with the picture and maybe hold the image to be interpreted behind their back and then show it every now and again.

Quick tip

Get the students to assess their own or another student's piece of work. This can be done either with or without the success criteria at the start. At first, it can be good to not use the success criteria, since it means they will have to discuss the problem in a more open way. The success criteria can then be shown at the end to round up the activity.

E1T1; 5, 4, 3, 2, 1; or 5, 3,1;

Or any Other Acronym You Like

Here is explanation some of the acronyms:

- **Everyone (E1) Tell/Teach One (T1) or E1T1**
  - Everybody must tell someone one skill/fact they have learned today. This is usually done in a short time frame (like one minute) to keep the pace up.
- **5, 4, 3, 2, 1**
  - This is where the students reflect on a lesson by producing the number of facts on the tasks. For example: Name five senses; name four areas that used those senses; name three receptors and two stimuli. Draw one reflex arc for one of the stimuli and one receptor.
- **5, 3, 1**
  - Choose five core ideals of a subject, for example the Christian faith. Order the three most important; and for one factor, discuss why it is the most important.

Or just invent an acronym based on the subject taught. When it comes to acronyms like this, the most important aspect is that it must be used consistently to get into the students' heads.

The use of any of these acronyms allows the delivering of a discussion point to come up with a variety of answers as a result. This produces an element of an outstanding lesson, because it shows that students can reflect on their learning. They also show a resilience to challenge through group work and cross-curricular skills.

Literacy Ideas That Can Be Problematic

It is important to recognise that some ideas are most likely never to be seen in an outstanding lesson, especially with older students, because they lack the necessary challenge. Examples of which include:

Gap fills—In general, they don't get the student to think. Gap fills just get them to comprehend what word fits the sentence. It doesn't answer the question, "Why does the word fit the sentence?" Where is the deeper learning? The worst ones are where the first letters are also given. Avoid this where possible since there is very little comprehension.

Word search—It takes some students thirty seconds and others ten minutes; what are they actually learning?

Quick tip

Avoid any activity that does not use keywords/phrases/skills as its basis. This is always the first focus in terms of literacy in every subject.

Numeracy

Like literacy, numeracy can also be split into simple and easy to follow rules. In lessons, there are elements of numeracy which teachers just don't realise they are using, so it is helpful to ask some simple questions to highlight the numeracy around us. For example:

"Are there calculations, however simple (multiply, divide, add, subtract, etc.)?"

"Is data being represented in any form (e.g. graph, table, bar chart)?"

"Are numbers being used in anyway (whole, decimals, fractions)?"

"Is there recognition or manipulation of shapes?"

"Is data being interpreted in any way?"

If the answer to any or all of these is yes, then the lesson includes some numeracy. It is often hard to think of any numeracy in lessons like art or religious education (RE). However, at some point in art lessons, the students will be dealing with the numeracy skill of recognising two dimensional or three dimensional shapes. In RE, students may be looking at data. For example, the followers of religions or the growth of religions. There is numeracy and literacy for that matter, in most, and possibly, all lessons.

The starting point is just to be clear on what defines numeracy. This is helped by having an overall model of what numeracy looks like in the school. A good idea is to make sure the school has a common approach to numerical language (e.g. is it average or mean?) and if they don't, suggest it and run a focus group. If we all sing from the same hymn sheet, the learning will always improve.

When the overall numerical model has been developed, then explore the different numeracy techniques and see how they could fit into lessons. Here are a few to whet the appetite.

Three Number Shuffle

Get the students to pick three numbers and tell them to make any number by adding, subtracting, dividing, or multiplying. This can be supplemented by specifics. For example, students get the highest number, get the lowest, end on a prime number, or end with a number that is double the original total, etc. Also, relate the answer to the subject where possible.

Interpret a Chart/Graph

At higher ages especially, this can be an under-taught skill, which is frequently assessed in exams. In order to develop the skills; have clear questions and clear aims; and if it is possible to make a graph about a weird and wonderful thing, then it can be engaging as well. How about age versus toe nail length for a gross one to start off a lesson on growth? Consider the age of person versus the regular wearing of a hoodie. This is a great citizenship starter to discuss whether anti-social behaviour misconceptions are reality. By using these cross-curricular skills in all subjects, the maths and science teachers will love you for helping them out.

Make It Their Responsibility

As teachers, we present many parts in lessons where things like percentages and calculating averages are needed. For example, this can come up at the end of a test, a pop quiz, or even as an introduction to a topic. Are the students calculating their percentages and rounding up or down? If not, why aren't they?

Common Calculations Board

This is aboard for equations that are usually needed in every subject. Are the equations displayed so the students can refer to them when needed? For example, ensuring how to calculate percentages and how to round numbers is displayed. Even in an English classroom, students will need to calculate a percentage every now and again, so surprise them and have it on your wall.

Psychometric Shapes Tests

As a very quick starter, put a couple of psychometric test questions on the board and get your students to predict the next shape. This is very good practice for all students regardless of their age. As well, these questions are easily found on the Internet for different ages.

Random Shapes

Shapes can be used to develop a child's imagination in an open way, or link into a theme of the lesson as part of developing a "no fail" culture. The limit is again, the imagination, so let the ideas flow. It can be as simple as the shape below, what does this mean to you?

The children in this lesson came up with all these answers, showing how impressively open a child's mind is—something we as teachers should nurture.

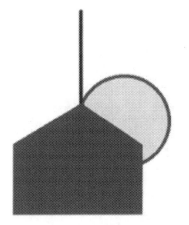

Answers:

A circle and a line
A house
A brown leaf next to a tree and a yellow ball
A house with a big TV aerial and a satellite dish
A yellow leaf next to a brown spade
A brown spade with a yellow ball behind it
A hanging house with a rising sun behind it
A tea bag and a slice of lemon
A pentagon and a line and a circle

Information Communication Technology (ICT)

ICT should be used to develop engagement and enhance creativity. At the same time, it is always good to make it part of the learning. I once saw computers out in a history lesson to make a table of facts in a lesson for twelve-year-olds. The two students I approached were working on the table and knew nothing about the skills behind it or the history. They spent twenty minutes making sure they had copied the facts and that it had the right colours. There are lessons to be gained here.

Firstly, for an outstanding lesson, avoid copying in any way unless it is new skill. For example, five-year-olds may need to put data into rows in an Excel spreadsheet because they are completely new to the software. However, twelve-year-olds will most probably have done it already, so where is the learning? So, here is the general rule: if your ICT task does not use skills in new way, or develop a new IT skill altogether, then don't do it.

The ICT must add to the learning and be an integral part of it. Thereby enhancing it and adding on some extra skill that the students can all learn.

Examples are listed below using Microsoft Excel, which may be used with any subject:

- ◦ Adding up totals using the simple sum function in Excel.
- ◦ Producing a mean from data gained in the lesson.
- ◦ Producing any form of chart using Excel.
- ◦ Producing a self-marking quiz using conditional formatting. It will go red or green for example, depending on whether the answer is right or wrong.

All of these include simple formulae, so any teacher can get to grips with it easily. If you are more ambitious, see the ICT teachers or technicians with an idea and see how they can be used to pimp a lesson.

 Visit http://sites.google.com/site/richardbyrnepdsite/home. It is a brilliant source of ideas and websites for ICT-based learning and there are a lot of useful websites on here so please go and have a look.

Online Corkboards

Online corkboards allow teachers to gather ideas from all of their students and see it quickly during a lesson. This can be as a starting point for discussion or homework where everybody feels they are contributing. All students can see each other's ideas and the teacher can move their comments around in an organisational way to get themes. The corkboard is live and changes almost instantaneously depending on your network speed. This means the students can see on their computer as well as on the main whiteboard. It is also good use as a motivator because many students will try and do it quickly so that their idea is original. The teacher can also make it tougher by saying every idea must be different. This is another idea where tablets can be used if there are class sets and several Post-it note-style apps that do the same job.

Quick tip

Wallwisher (www.wallwisher.com) is where it is free to log in, name the wall, and give the students the website address of the wall. They can then upload their comments which look like individual Post-it notes. Files, videos, and comments can all be put onto the wall, which is in public view.

Spaaze (www.spaaze.com) offers its users a board with an infinite space which resembles a virtual corkboard. Items can be placed on these boards. Currently, Spaaze offers seven different items: labels, notes, bookmarks, images, files, videos, and HTML. These items can be edited in place, moved via drag and drop, and positioned freely on the board. Therefore, it's possible to arrange a bunch of items any way you like.

When using corkboards, try and include aspects of the following:

- Name the wall with something characteristic of the class or the subject e.g. 10K2 or Poem If by Rudyard Kipling. This is helpful as the name is included in the web address for the wall.
- Use a wall as homework to prepare for the next lesson.
- Use as a great starting point for a discussion, say, using E1T1 or 5,3,1 or any other acronym.
- Use to gather thoughts and information very quickly during a lesson.

There are many virtual boards like Spaaze and Wallwisher where you can place online stickers or Post-it notes, which are all great for looking at ideas, sharing ideas between groups and with teachers. They are all engaging and have elements of differentiation. Where else can a lower-ability student see a higher-ability student's work and then be able to ask them about it? This creates a great forum for class discussion and possible debate.

Online Questionnaire/Polls

These can be used in lessons to gauge opinion through a questionnaire. Many subjects can use polls and since they are online, the results analysis is instant, visual, and interactive.

A website that is used by both teachers and students is Survey Monkey (www.surveymonkey.com). You can design and build your own surveys or choose from their templates, collect and choose how to distribute and start collecting responses, and analyse and use their analytical tools, having full compatibility with Excel.

Creating Your Own Website

Why not get the students to create their own website or host information on a site built by the teacher, teaching assistant, or technician? It doesn't have to be an ICT lesson to do this; the website can be on anything. There are loads of free websites that offer this capability in a simple way, so there is no need to be an ICT expert to engage with them.

Look at the two examples underneath that allow students to make their own website for free:

kidswebsitecreator.com, and www.webnode.com.

Microsoft Office

Since Office is the general package used in almost any school, it is our job, whatever subject we are currently teaching, to use technology such as Word, PowerPoint, Publisher, Access, and Excel. These packages are only mentioned because they are widespread in school. Of course there are other packages, too, but they are sparser in education.

In terms of teaching with ICT, here are some simple themes for using Office:

- **Keep it simple**—At the most, get the students to use one or two new ICT techniques, otherwise they will take a long time. This can mean that pace and timings can go out the window.

- **No copying and pasting (unless involving images)**—This avoids the copying of large pieces of text which the students often don't fully understand. By making this rule, the students have to read it and comprehend the information. The images are the only exception, so can be copied, but they still need to be explained. By explaining, students are using the skills of analysis and interpretation, which is a high level skill and always part of an outstanding lesson.

- **Think ahead, is the Internet needed?**—Get the technicians to switch off the Internet in the room if there is no need to use it. This means there is less chance for distraction and disruption.

- **Strict time limits**—Use overt, clear, and achievable time limits to avoid distraction from the Internet.

- **Words**—Limit the amount of words overall or in each section, so the students have to think more and do less copying of text.

- **Keywords or phrases**—Indicate which key terms are to be used and make it the students' job to explain them in context.

- **Examples of strict success criteria**:
  1. I am looking for you to create a one-slide poster to explain . . . on PowerPoint.
  2. It must contain a range of 170-200 words which must include the keywords: . . .
  3. There is no copying and pasting other than images imported.

- **Give one simple ICT focus + Lesson content**—For example: they may be new to importing photos, so this is their ICT focus for this lesson in the context of the subject taught (e.g. explaining Roman developments in Britain). Remember to judge the ICT focus by assessing the children. By talking to them (or their ICT teacher) it is possible to find out what they know about ICT and so plan an effective ICT slant to a lesson.

- **Formulas: Why not?**—Try using a formula with Excel. Don't just make a table for inputting data. For example, if the students are doing experiments, get them to manipulate the data by using a formula or producing a graph.

- **Explore the macros with Word**—Find out what the main uses of the programs are to both help the teacher and the students. For example, in Word, find out what subscript and superscript are; determine what styles consist of; learn the meaning of content pages; determine which wizards would be helpful; learn about templates; find out how the equation editor can be used.

- **Explore the macros with PowerPoint**—Why not reject the standard PowerPoint Presentation approach? Get the students to fiddle with timings and animation whilst doing the lesson. By doing this it develops their understanding of PowerPoint and the subject as a dual purpose.

- **Presentations guidelines**—Make everyone contribute.
  - For example:
    - One student narrates.
    - One student acts out a scene.
    - One student does the introduction.
    - One student does the summary.

Quick tip

See if the leader in your school will fund the Microsoft Office Specialist (MOS) course which trains teachers to be a comparative expert on Microsoft in your school and, thereby, enhances your professional development opportunities.

With all of these formats, regardless of whether you wish to or can do the MOS course, learn as much as possible about teaching with ICT. The opportunity that ICT presents is huge for both the teacher and the students, especially with the advent of tablets in modern teaching.

Video Cameras

Video cameras area fantastic tool in lessons as long as there is permission for taking images of students from their parents. This is best done through a whole-school permission slip. Check this is signed before videos are used in lesson since it can be a minefield otherwise. The applications of video are almost endless, but here are some suggestions which can be used in a lesson on a regular basis.

Movie Maker—This is another package that is free and easy to use where students use video cameras to make a video of their own. This package can be used with most of the ideas below. From the youngest to the oldest, students find it useful and can do it easily, so, just get a friendly IT teacher or technician to show you how.

Homework—Allow students to take video and/or pictures of their lesson and then use them to help them produce their homework, for example, writing a blog/news report, adding to their website, or just writing a magazine article/diary. If there is an area that all students can access, for example, an area of the VLE, then the teacher can load pictures up quickly during the lesson so the students can access them at home.

Praise—If a student has done something brilliant, allow him or her to take a picture with a mobile phone or tablet (if available or allowed in the school) and send it to the student's parents/carers. This is great for praise, but it's usually best to do this at the end of the lesson so no time is wasted.

Photo Presentation Questions—Many programs/apps can create simple photo presentations allowing the addition of simple transitions, effects, and music, to photos. One of the most practical programs is Microsoft Photo Story, which is fantastically simple.

Pick an effect, and Photo Story does most of the application itself. For example, take a picture of a piece of work or students working, download the pictures to the computer and place it into Photo Story. Within a couple of minutes key questions can be added related to that picture. When presenting, it also possible to focus in on certain areas.

Quick tip

For those with access to tablets, apps can be used to create a similar effect but through a comic strip. The easiest apps for this purpose are Strip Design (£1.99), Comic Puppets Lite (Free), and Bubble—Speech Bubbles & Text Photo (Free), which can all produce comic strips with photos/speech bubbles and some with animations drawn on the app.

Prezi—This is presentation software that opens up a new world between whiteboards and slides. Using the software, it is possible to literally zoom into parts of the lesson on the canvas. Images/videos/YouTube can be imported to create the Prezi presentation, however, there are many Prezi files already freely available on the website (www.prezi.com). It makes it fun to explore ideas and the connections between them. The result is that presentations are visually captivating and stand apart from standard PowerPoint. The good thing is that it's free; however, this does mean that files are stored online. Try producing lessons using Prezi or even better, get the students to produce their work using Prezi.

Green Screen Technology—Green screen allows the students to place themselves in front of any background such as the Wild West or a snowboarding backdrop. There are limitless ideas for this, but think of the simple ones like writing news & reviews, creation of a storyboard to do with any subject. Maybe do *Dragons Den* in this way, allow the students to be in complete control of the filming and the background. These skills ignite the imagination and make the children dream of careers in the media.

 Quick tip — Look to be innovative and see if you can get a green screen set up in your school. It can cost as little as £1000. There are still many funding opportunities out there where the money may be sourced or requested from school leaders.

Microphones, Audacity, and Transcriptions

It can be very difficult to persuade shy children to use the cameras because they can be self-conscious and parents may not want their child filmed. To overcome this problem and get everybody to access technology in lessons, many students prefer to do audio recording as it is slightly less daunting. If a microphone is available and can connect to the PC at school, it is very easy to record students' discussions and to play it back to them for further development discussion and other teaching ideas.

Quick tip — If you are really up for a challenge, then download Audacity. This is a free programme on the Internet that can be used to edit sound and splice different parts together. This is another skill to be learned and can be used to add depth to the learning in a lesson.

Chapter 4:
TEACHING EPISODES

In any outstanding lesson, there is always a need to refocus efforts on independent learning and challenge. Visualise a lesson where students are focused on their learning and know how they can improve. Achieving this is not always easy. Different teaching techniques require regular practice to make them successful with different classes and ability levels. However, by adapting techniques to the teacher's own individual style, students will develop confidence in their teacher, confidence in themselves, and a willingness to have a go at anything with which they are faced.

Always have the focus on the learning, but in order to make students do the work, we need to lay the foundations of good teaching practice. In this chapter, we lay those foundations and use basic building blocks of good teaching. The effort throughout is to move away from the traditional view of a teacher standing at the front lecturing.

The teacher lecturing for most of the lesson is commonly referred to as "chalk and talk" or didactic teaching. This is where the students are usually listening and watching, which must be at a minimum for good learning to take place. The aim is for students to do as much "learning by doing" as possible.

Learn by Doing

Wherever possible and whatever the subject, students should be learning by doing. All lessons include a vast variety of different techniques such as reading/writing/teaching others, etc. No techniques should be used in isolation, but in combination.

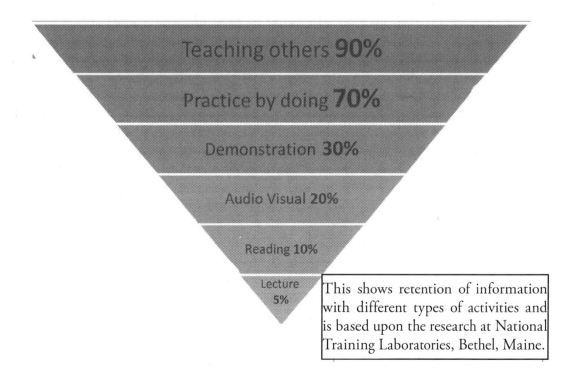

Teaching others **90%**

Practice by doing **70%**

Demonstration **30%**

Audio Visual **20%**

Reading **10%**

Lecture **5%**

This shows retention of information with different types of activities and is based upon the research at National Training Laboratories, Bethel, Maine.

The emphasis should always be:

"How can the teacher get the students to take responsibility?"

The reason for this being, that according to research at Maine Laboratories, retention of information is higher where students take responsibility for their own learning. For example, 90 per cent retention if a student has taught other children or immediately used the information, 75 per cent if they have learned by doing, and 50 per cent if they have learned in the form of a discussion.

This falls markedly to 5 per cent if they are being lectured. So we go back to the tip above, avoid chalk and talk where possible and always get the students to "do" whenever possible. Have this attitude when planning and the students will become more independent as a result.

The following is a list of various different techniques that can be used to facilitate learning by doing.

- **Clock watcher**—Keep a clock or watch handy and time yourself, or even better, get a student to time the lesson. This may feel uncomfortable at first, however, give it a try. You will find that it will sharpen the timings in lessons and maintain the pace.

- **Responsibility on the students**—Let the students have a chance to discuss your subject and come up with ideas during the teaching episode whenever possible.

- **3B4Me, C3B4Me, etc.**—There are 4 Bs that are used in this method. They are Buddy, Book, Brain, and Boss, which is converted into an easily understood text style. Either use Three Before Me (3B4Me), or See Three Before Me (C3B4Me). Promote the students in researching, reflecting, and questioning themselves (their Brain, their Book), their peers (their Buddy) and the teacher (their Boss) by using this approach in the classroom. The Brain, Buddy, and Book are the three areas a student must research before they ask the teacher (the Boss) a question. This develops their self-reliance and communicative skills, which sets the expectations from the beginning. It is useful to have a poster of this in the room, which sets the standard from the beginning. Many images are available on the Internet. Just look up 3B4Me or C3B4Me.

- **Engagement is variety**—Choose a variety of techniques (over all parts of a lesson) to maintain interest. A student who is engaged in learning will not stay engaged if they do the same techniques every lesson.

- **Humour**—Students are just like any other person; if they are laughing, they are enjoying the lesson. If they are enjoying the lesson, they are engaged and learning more. Don't confuse this with trying to be funny—teachers aren't comedians. It just means have a sense of humour, see the lighter side where possible, and let your personality come through.

- **Relevance**—This will get students to remember what is being taught and initiate their memory. For example, a smell of a certain food will initiate people's memories. As will finding the relevance of a subject in everyday life, or for that matter, in a specific child's life. For this reason, it is important that we engage with students and get to know them in our subjects and in a wider context. Consider a simple example: if a student works on cars at the weekend, use mechanical aspects in a variety of ways in explanations.

- **No hands policy**—Try and do a mostly no hands policy where questions are asked, instead, directly use the child's name. It is incredibly important that teachers learn the names of all students as soon as possible, since this makes them feel valued and results in less behavioural problems.

- **Get videoed**—This is going to sound strange, but get involved in school development of teaching and learning by being videoed whilst teaching. This is usually to help with career professional development and training. Watch the video back, only then can some people realise how much time they take talking. Teaching outstanding lessons is as much about self-evaluation and reflection as it is about anything else.

- **Talking**—Try to talk roughly between 100 and 120 words per minute. Practice in front of the mirror, and time yourself. Have you ever tried to listen to someone who is talking too slow or too fast? It's either a nightmare for comprehension and/or boring.

- **Clear focus**—Start with a clear focus on what must be taught traditionally to the students and what can be learned independently. Use any opportunities where the students can discover or work out the answer by themselves.

- **Success criteria**—What success criteria are related to the teaching? What is expected to be shown during the lesson to display progress? These questions can help the design of the hinge point question(s) in the lesson.

The techniques above are designed to help develop teaching practice along central themes of learning by doing. The next section describes different teaching techniques or resources that can be used in the teaching phase or beforehand.

Modelling and Role Plays

"I only remember electricity because you made us run around the room as electrons."

This quote was from a student who was asked about role plays and whether they helped her learn. The response speaks for itself. Well-executed role plays amounts to learning by doing. There are other reasons for doing a role play such as, student participation, engagement, and an element of kinaesthetic learning (physical or tactile learning). All that is needed is a context and the teacher's imagination and passion to design the teaching sequences.

As a suggestion, try learning about the following with a role play:

- Mining for metals before and after the industrial revolution
- Plants soaking up different nutrients and growing
- Deprivation in the cities in the 1800's
- Life of any influential historical figure

See which technique could fit in your lesson:

- **Student-Led Modelling of a Principle**
  - The students lead and develop their role play in an independent way. Successful student-led role plays are linked to clear differentiated learning objectives or success criteria.
  - Consider an example where students were acting as particles in a science lesson. They create a role play modelling particles within a solid, a liquid, and a gas. The clear differentiated success criteria allow them to know the direction their role play had to go and so, in this way, they had some responsibility for their learning. The success criteria were also used by the teams to assess each other's performance and peer assess.

- **Teacher-Led Modelling of a Principle**
  - In teacher-led modelling, the teacher clearly instructs a small set of students on how to demonstrate a principle to the class. During this instruction, the teacher asks the class, as a whole, questions based around this principle. Be aware that for an outstanding lesson, this must be short and very much to the point so the entire lesson does not become teacher led.

- **Three Shot Showdown**
  - Get students to describe the learning for the lesson at any point by acting out three freeze frame pictures. The students are normally the only props, however, it is really up to the teacher; props can be added if appropriate and available. As freeze frame suggests, the students don't move; there are just three picture shots as if they were camera shots.

Quick
tip
This can be combined with photo presentation software, such as Microsoft Photo Story, allowing you to present other peoples' work on the screen and ask questions if you want to spice it up in an ICT way. Photo Story is a free download from the Internet, so just ask a friendly IT technician to download it if you are unsure.

The Power of Analogy

An outstanding teacher is always thinking of a way to explain a difficult concept to students. This is called "reshaping the learning" in the Framework and is an incredibly important teaching skill.

One effective method of explanation is to create an analogy. For those unfamiliar, this is a similarity between like features of two things upon which a comparison may be based. A classic one is the analogy between the heart and a pump. When constructing analogies, try and do it in the simplest way possible, relating it to the student's or class' experience. Reshaping explanations are crucial when presenting information in any teaching sequence, so make sure there is an analogy or two already thought up.

Emphasis

Get the students to highlight key points all the time. This leads back into preparation. Ensure there are highlighters handy in the AfL Box. If this is not possible, then be imaginative and get the students to place a star around important words or sections. Always do things in a memorable way that is unique to you as a teacher.

Consider a space lesson on the electromagnetic spectrum. This example below, donated by a teacher who was using blue for the "U" and red for all the other letters. Here is the dingbat or rebus puzzle that was used to emphasise a key point. What do you think it means?

$$\text{uNIVERSE}$$

Students remembered this because it's a little bit different and in this case, a little bit wacky. The answer is: "The Expanding Universe". The extension was that red shift refers to the expansion of the universe, so all the expanded letters were red. Blue shift refers to the universe contracting, hence the smallest letter, "U", was blue. The teacher used this to ask questions and develop a lesson on the topic in a very skilful way.

Another example of emphasis in a similar lesson is when an equation was being used and the key component, "m", needs to be considered. See what questions the same teacher posed below:

"Kinetic energy is constant for all particles and can be considered as one. What determines the velocity of the particles? Use the equations to explain."

$$k.e = 1/2 \, m v^2$$

$$\sqrt{\frac{2k.e}{m}} = V$$

In terms of teaching ideas, the point is not to understand the science, so don't worry if you don't. Here the physics teacher wanted them to know, "Velocity (V) is increased in Mass Spectrometry by the mass of a fragment (m)". So to emphasise, the "*m*" was made large, stating that "*m*" made the biggest effect, but importantly, not explaining why. The teacher allowed some independent thinking time and then launched into explaining the equation and the significance of "*m*" on kinetic energy, always first seeing whether anyone else could explain it first. This always put the emphasis on the students to learn and not always the teacher to teach.

A similar emphasis technique can be done with keywords in different subjects. Keep it as simple as ringing or underlining the words that are important. Emphasis is an effective technique for students who have English as an additional language (**EAL**) so that they can use their dictionaries to quickly look up the words if necessary.

Quick tip

Tablets or smartphones are also great to use with EAL students so they can quickly use translator apps. There are several free ones, such as Google/ Bing Translate or *i*Translate.

Group Work Methods

Group work is integral because it involves independence and collaboration in its core. There are two main types of group work: a model based upon similar abilities or groups based upon mixed abilities. Both will work in differing situations, so it's up to the teacher when and where they work best.

Closed Activities

Closed activities are essentially where the answer is non-negotiable, which is very common in maths or numeracy lessons. In group work situations, if the answers are closed, then it can be best to have all the higher-ability students together. This means motivation can improve and competition is initiated. This will all be held together using clear and challenging time limits with success criteria and/or self-assessment for the work.

It is important to emphasise "can be" because really, all of the teaching decisions in this area are based upon the students. As long as there is adequate challenge and progress for everyone, then the groupings should be correct. It is the teacher's knowledge of the students which decides which is the best groupings. The above suggestion is only a guide; use knowledge of the class and imagination to make the decision.

Open Activities

An open activity is where there are selections of different answers to a task or a problem. All of the questions or tasks could have various effective solutions which could solve the problem. This means that each question can require different abilities and different strengths to answer. This is where mixed ability could be the way forward.

Open activities are a great way to motivate groups of students who are not normally good at a subject. They may be a good at the wider learning, such as leadership, literacy, numeracy, or ICT but feel that they aren't good at this subject. Take a look at their skills and make sure the tasks set involve these abilities. This means the student will become more engaged in the lesson. They will also be empowered by successfully working at a higher level and knowing that they have been able to contribute. Challenge can happen in different ways, and wider learning can be used to develop your tasks to a higher level.

Quick tip
Roles and responsibilities are essential for successful group work, so make clear each member's responsibility. Who is the scribe, if you have one? Who is presenting the work? Who is narrating? Who chairs the discussion? Look into the differentiation chapter for ideas.

Does the Teacher Choose, or Do the
Students Choose Their Groups?

Seating Plans

Seating plans are always a good idea in lessons. However, they need to be kept fresh by changing them every six weeks, or every term. This allows the development of a classroom environment where everyone mingles and talks to each other. It is also clear to see who works well next to each other.

Seating plans can be begun by organising them boy/girl on the first day and always referring to the learning behaviour as the main influence of the seating plan. By referring to the learning when the seating plan is changed, many difficult conversations can be avoided. Maybe ask them, "Are you learning well next to that person?"

This can be continued throughout the year, hopefully, ending in an arrangement of students based around the best learning. It is also used as a praise mechanism. For example, after a couple of changes to the seating plan, if they have been working well, it may be time to ask, "Where do you want to sit?"

It may be possible to hand over some responsibility to the students because they will know by this point, and they will only stay there if they are working well and achieving their best. If it does not work; change it back.

Seating plans have such a good impact on the decision-making process when determining groups. Seating plans can help answer the questions to choose or not to choose certain groupings. If seating plans are based upon learning, it will mean that the groups will be ready to work well in their current groups regardless of the activity chosen.

The details of the seating plan are down to the teacher, but here are some different ways to set up seating plans:

- Choose to have groups of higher achievers in the opposite corners if they need to work in similar ability groupings. This still allows easy mixing if needed.
- For mixed ability, spread them around and find out how the students work together. As the plan is refined, get the best pairings/groups of workers next to each other, not necessarily being led by ability.
- Sometimes friendship groups are actually good learning groups. If so, then let the students choose their groups. This will get the students working together whilst gaining more responsibility.

Quick tip For those with a special interest in seating plans and more learning games; try out the ideas on developing in collaborative learning by Kagan at www.kaganonline.com.

Diamond Nine

The Diamond Nine is a process by which different areas of teaching are on labelled cards. Trainees decide upon the most significant to have an outstanding lesson using a Diamond Nine formation as shown in the diagram. The area that has the highest significance in terms of the question is placed at the top and the significance lowers as you go down.

Just do the same with students, for example can you do the following exercise:

"What were the likely causes of the First World War?"

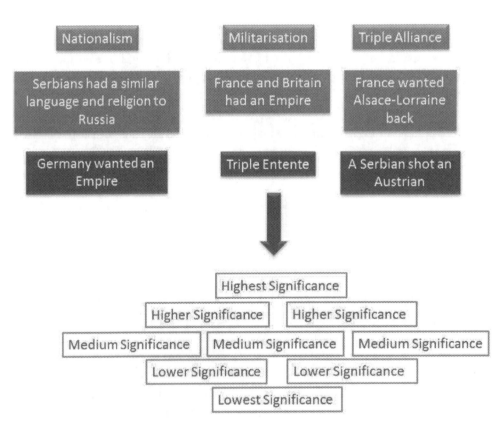

So go on and try the Diamond Nine. Begin the debate and design it on any subject you want.

The TASC Wheel

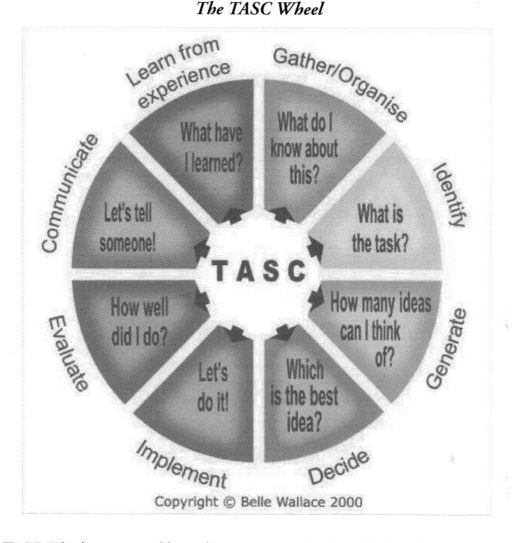

Copyright © Belle Wallace 2000

The TASC Wheel, a great problem-solving resource, which can be found in various guises at www.tascwheel.com, and kindly donated by permission of Belle Wallace.

TASC stands for Thinking Actively in a Social Context (TASC). The TASC wheel is a step-by-step process by which students work through open-ended challenges in groups and come up with solutions. The TASC Wheel is essentially a list of key questions to be considered in turn, when approaching a task. It can be used as an effective teaching strategy for developing problem-solving skills in a clear and structured way. If used consistently, it can also develop independent learning skills across all subjects. The students can use the TASC Wheel to work through a problem in small groups often using a central piece of A3 paper. The TASC Wheel actively encourages students to be creative by working methodically through challenges much like the Outstanding Lesson Framework. Thus avoiding the times where challenges are given and students just don't know where to start. As with any successful technique, a class has to be coached in its use, so try it gradually and do a few sections of the wheel in lessons. Eventually, the class will thrive on it and display independent learning abilities. For further information on the TASC Wheel, visit www.tascwheel. com where various resources are available to help deliver structured independent learning.

Logovisual—A Way to Develop Independent Thinking

Logovisual is a website which highlights the use of Logovisual technology and creative thinking using hexagon-shaped writing tools. Logovisual tools come in the form of hexagonal sticky notes and magnetic hexagons. The advantage for the notes is that they have a double sticky pad on the back so do not curl up when attached to a board or table. The hexagonal shapes fit together in a honeycomb structure and come in a variety of colours. Here is an idea using Logovisual again to whet the appetite:

- **Stimulating and grouping ideas**—Imagine a lesson with an overarching concept or discussion point where students need to contribute as many ideas as possible.
  - Give out, for example, five yellow hexagonal notes and get students to think individually of ideas by writing one per note, then sticking them on the table. This is a great way to introduce a topic where everyone can contribute. They also develop independent thoughts in a no-fail scenario.
  - In teams, students group together similar ideas.
  - Teams are then given green notes which are used to label these groups giving an overall title to each set of ideas.
  - By doing this, Logovisual tools can effectively start discussions and help plan essays or summaries in a coherent and visual manner.

Imagine the potential. What about introducing a topic on any one of the following using this method:

- *Hamlet* by Shakespeare or any other plays for that matter
- History of Northern Ireland's troubles or, again, any other topic in history
- The origin of global warming
- Keywords or ideas linked to France, Mexico, Ireland, Canada, etc.

For more information on Logovisual thinking and how it can help in teaching, visit www. logovisual.com.

Square It

This is a great way of doing mixed-ability group work where open-ended questions are given with every student giving/justifying an opinion. Imagine posing this question: "Who agrees with capital punishment?"

Now, get the students to stand in a straight line; those who totally agree are one end, and those who totally disagree are at the other end. Everyone who is in between lines up according to what degree each agrees with the statement. This means they must discuss it as they go along.

Here is the key: bend the line so that those who totally agree face those who totally disagree. Next, bend each line again and form a square. Each line of the square enters into a debate over their opinions with the line standing opposite. There is now an opportunity for students of opposing views to start a discussion and a committed debate. The following groups result:

1. Those who totally agree face those who partially disagree
2. Those who totally disagree face those who partially agree

In this way, each group justifies their opinions with other students with opposing views, and hopefully a lively debate will ensue. Literally, the line can be moved in whatever way to get different people of different views facing off.

Chapter 5:
ENGAGING QUESTIONING TECHNIQUES

In an outstanding lesson, every student is fully part of both the learning and the class. This is achieved through consistent communication with every student, which is mostly delivered through questioning. Questioning is a part of the lesson, which can be exciting for students and gives them a chance to get thinking. It is, however, not to be confused with hinge point questions and plenaries, because questioning is usually one to one or one to group. Hinge point questions and plenaries are whole-class assessments in order that the teacher can find out where the learning is within the whole class. Hinge points and plenaries will be discussed later. For now, we'll go through simple questioning techniques that enhance the fun and get students to think.

All of these techniques are carried out to make sure there is "no opt out" in your classroom. For there to be outstanding learning, all students must progress. Therefore, all students should know there is no option but to be involved. Couple the questioning with a lot of praise. In that way, students will enjoy each technique and look forward to them. Please refer to the Assessment for Learning box mentioned earlier for any of the resources that are used in these techniques in Chapter 1: "Meet and Greet."

The Ball

This is a technique where a ball is thrown to get students to answer questions. Why not use students' initial apprehension to answer questions in order to develop excitement? Throw the ball at the students, and if they catch it, they don't answer a question. Remember, the situation is engineered by the teacher, who can make a student answer a question by throwing it a bit harder or more awkwardly. All students love the ball technique, and all will be on tenterhooks watching for it, which equates to maximum engagement.

Quick tip

Change the rules depending on the class. If all are eager, flip the rules so that if the students catch the ball, they answer a question. Change it according to how the students are, and any class will enjoy it.

Alphabet Cards or Random Letters

Use the alphabet cards in the AfL box and get a student to pick up a card with a letter of the alphabet on it. The student who has the surname beginning with that letter answers the question. Or alternatively, if there are no cards, then get the students to give a letter of the alphabet. Don't tell them whether cards are being chosen based on surnames, or first names, or even the second letter, or third letter of the name. This means it is totally random to the students. This is, of course, a con. The teacher is in control since he or she knows the students' names and can engineer who to choose.

Random Numbers

Similar to the alphabet cards or random letters, just get the students to choose a number, then start the count on a random person and count through students in turn to find who answers the question.

For example, if the number is six, then count six people down the row and ask the question of number six. The teacher is absolved of all blame. If a student complains that he or she has been picked, blame it on the person who chose the number. Genius!

Random Name Generators

One such programme is called "The Hat", which can be downloaded from the Internet. Enter the students' names using an Excel spreadsheet (this can be taken from registration software), and "The Hat" program generates a random name when a button is pressed.

Extra Lives

Get students to answer a question. If they are unable to answer it properly, they are allowed to ask only one other person to help them. Try to make it so the helper student assists the student with the question but does not necessarily reveal the answer. This makes it more challenging.

No Hands and All Answering!

This is a technique to get in at the start of every term or year. As soon as the students walk in, inform them that everybody will answer a question by the end of the lesson and immediately say, "No hands are going up." Make it clear as well that some may get asked twice. This builds an atmosphere again where no one is left out and all start actively paying attention. It can also be combined with group work or Think-Pair-Square-Share (where students think of ideas individually and share it eventually in a group of four).

Finish My Sentence . . .

This involves active listening at its best. Ask a question that requires a longer answer, then say to everyone, "Listen carefully, because I will say your name to start the answer; and then once I say another person's name, they must continue the answer."

Cycle this three to four times. Everybody actively listens because they may be next, and they must know what has been said to continue the sentence/answer.

Split the Room

Split the room into two halves typically by running an imaginary line down the middle. Now, get the students from one half to pick students to answer questions from the other half. It is a very quick and easy method needing no resources.

Change the sides asking questions as often as is necessary to keep the pace going. Quickly decide which person will be answering and students will either be very eager or try to hide away and blaming their friends if they get picked. Even though this is so, this technique is always good natured.

Close Your Eyes and Who Is It?

Get the whole class to close their eyes, preferably while in a circle and not on stools (since they are noisy). Tap one person on the shoulder, and they can then open their eyes, get up, and tap another person's shoulder to ask a question or answer a question. To make it exciting, the kids must guess who the person tapping was at the end.

The Questioner

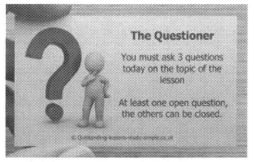

Here is another one of the differentiation cards. Give the questioner card out at the start of the lesson to a student who must ask three questions during the lesson. In this example, it is set to one open and two closed questions. This is available from our website.

This is another opportunity to differentiate. For example, if the person is of higher ability, use all open questions.

Students Ask the Question, Not You!

Get the students to quickly make up three questions on the topic either at the start, middle, or end of the lesson. For a more challenging session, let them choose open or closed questions.

For a lower-ability group of students, give them the keywords and get them to do questions. They can then "split the room" to ask each other. Always encourage them to make it as difficult as possible and see how much the students want to make it difficult for each other. However, be aware of the pitfalls; make it clear to the student asking that they must be able to answer the questions they ask.

Jeopardy

Jeopardy takes a bit of practice to get the children's heads behind it. Jeopardy is a game where a quiz is reversed. The question becomes the answer; the answer becomes the question. This can be a bit confusing.

So, for example:

Question: "I live in the water and can be different shades of brown and green."

Answer: "What is a frog?"

Develop this by giving more than one clue and making it a competition. How about making a rule that the earlier the student gets the answer, the more points they get? It is very easy to do. Think of the answer ("What is a frog?") but with five clues this time:

- Clue Question 1: "I live in the water."
- Clue Question 2: "I can be different shades of brown and green."
- Clue Question 3: "I sometimes have spots."
- Clue Question 4: "I live on land and water."
- Clue Question 5: "I give birth to tadpoles."

The earlier the student gives the answer "What is a Frog?", the more points he or she gets. This can even be combined with a sticky note. Instruct them that when they think they have got the answer to write it on a sticky note on the desk. This must face away from them (for example, on their pencil cases), where the teacher can see it while the person in front of them can't.

Back-to-Back Pictionary

Get the students to sit back to back, with one facing the wall and the other facing the main teaching whiteboard. On the main whiteboard, place a clue to a word or key phrase. The students facing the whiteboard tell the student behind how to draw an interpretation of this keyword or phrase. In doing so, they must not use the keyword or phrase. The teacher then asks all of the students facing away from the board to show their boards. They must not look at the main whiteboard.

The teacher can then use it to assess the students and find out what they know about this keyword/phrase. This is such a fun activity and can work as a small starter or some simple assessment to make sure everybody understands the keyword of a lesson.

Chapter 6:
HINGE POINT QUESTIONS

As the name "hinge point question" indicates, it is a question that has answers that can take the lesson in at least two different directions. The directions of the lesson are, therefore, dependent upon the teacher's assessment of the students' understanding. For a direction to be determined, a hinge point question must be based on an important concept in a lesson. This concept must be crucial for the students to understand before the teacher moves on in the lesson. By assessing for this purpose, a teacher can make a striking impact on learning-by-delivering-tailored teaching to each individual student using the Outstanding Lesson Framework.

In the Framework, the hinge point question comes after the teaching episode and is meant to assess the skills, which are to be practiced in the differentiated tasks. This allows the teacher to give out differentiated activities/roles as well as help students who don't clearly understand the learning in the lesson.

The characteristics of a good hinge point question are as follows:

- A hinge point question falls, at the very latest, halfway through a lesson, depending on the independent nature of your lesson, or it may come earlier.
- It should take no longer than a minute to ask.
- It takes no longer than two minutes for students to respond.
- The answers must be easily interpreted by the teacher within approximately thirty seconds.
- All students can respond to it simultaneously.
- Questions are designed in a way that makes it very difficult to guess. This means the students get the answer right for the right reason.
- Make the questions so that in the end not everyone gets it right. In this way, the students can be differentiated appropriately and the right work or help delivered.
- There can be more than one question.

This is the teacher's opportunity to see where everybody is in the class at a snapshot in time. They can then use this information to give out activities tailored to the student's individual needs and talents. In an outstanding lesson, the assessment is throughout, but here is the chance to make sure the students recognise what they are doing. It can also help you deliver the reason behind why they are doing it, which can allow you to describe the next step in their learning.

Practical Challenges of a Hinge Point Question

The common challenge amongst teachers when it comes to hinge point questions is the following:

- It can be difficult to write them. This is because the questions need to be sufficiently challenging so the students cannot guess the answer. The good news is that this gets easier with time and practice.
- Stopping the students from copying each other.

In this chapter we will describe the hinge point, talking through the questions themselves and giving some general logistical advice for setting them up. There are many ways of doing them, so make sure the assessment techniques are varied all the time. This keeps students engaged, because the assessment is no different to the rest of the lesson. Vary it as often as possible and use the resources in the Assessment for Learning box.

Mini-Whiteboards (MWBs)

MWBs are by far the most useful way of delivering hinge points. Unfortunately, they can sometimes be used to less than their full potential; so here are some simple guidelines to ensure success:

- **Up at the Same Time**—Use pace and imagination in the delivery to get the MWBs all up at the same time. Think of a keyword to get this happening that suits your style and personality. Take a look at the following examples and imagine how they could be vocally embellished to get students to raise up the answers quickly. Remember volume, tempo, pace, and pitch:

  ○ 5, 4, 3, 2, 1—Up, up, up, up, up!
  ○ Boards Up—Go, go, go!
  ○ Show me, show me, show me, people!
  ○ These can all be made catchy and easy to recognise by students if used consistently.

- **Eyes Open**—Look for who isn't putting their board up quickly. Make sure they are approached afterwards to make sure they are not copying.

- **Short or Visual Answers**—Always develop a question that involves only a number, letter, a few words, a diagram, or a picture as an answer. Assessment should be complete within approximately thirty seconds, and this cannot be done with long answers that take too long to read.

- **Group Them**—When assessing, look for groupings of answers and scan quickly. This allows quick assessment of all the similar ones which will normally be the right answer.

- **Logistics**—How do you manage this to get it done quickly?

  ○ Do not have pens out all lesson unless you trust your class. They can be a distraction.
  ○ Have whiteboards at their desks ready all the time.
  ○ Get students to give out pens, since it is quicker.
  ○ Or do it a bit differently: avoid a free for all when they all get their resources by having differing board monitors or a note on the board as they walk in: "Ben, Becky, Olivia, John get the boards and pens out, please."

- **Encourage Privacy**—In an observation of a teacher, this short story about a new born baby was used to make the students keep their answer private: "Imagine your board is a new born baby, where would you keep it? Of course, close to your chest and hugging it tightly. Treat your whiteboard like a new born baby; make sure no one copies."

- **Simple Clues**—Look for copying and simple clues like a student delaying and turning slightly. This often means they are looking for inspiration from others. Singling out that person isn't positive, so make a mental note and come back to them later.

- **Consistency**—Use MWBs often, approximately every six lessons since students will get used to getting them out and doing it quickly, without getting bored of them.

ABCD Cards

ABCD cards allow the students to show a letter to the teacher and provide their answer to a multiple choice question, and as such, are an essential element for the Assessment for Learning box.

Producing them is a simple process; just use a word processor to write out the ABCD, print onto card and chop up for a full class set of cards. For ease, sets can be placed into envelopes or on key ties so each student has their own cards. This is a great resource that is easy to give out and get in.

 Quick tip For a good wakeup call, if a lesson is starting to slow down, use ABCD corners. ABCD corners are just large cards with the A, B, C, and D in the corners of your classroom—cards which have the added advantage of making the students get up and move to the answer.

ABCD cards allow the teacher to get the students to answer prepared multiple choice hinge point questions. Don't be lulled into false first impressions; multiple choice questions are not necessarily lower challenge. Multiple choice answers can easily be designed by using techniques like we have already mentioned:

- Find the fib.
- Find the truth.
- Make all answers correct in order to make the students think.
- Make sure the multiple choice answers do not involve the answer at all.

All these techniques can be used to keep the students guessing and raise the challenge when assessing.

When using ABCD, avoiding copying between students can be challenging, so here are some hints to help you stop those cheating:

- **ABCD Cards**
  - Give out the cards and get each student to arrange their cards face down in a different order on the table. For example: BACD, BCDA, CABD. Ask the question to the whole class. The student who knows where his cards are and what order they are in will not hesitate. The student who obviously delays is more than likely confused, or trying to copy. This technique will eliminate most of the copying as students don't know each other's orders.

- **ABCD Corners**
  - Get the students to go to the corners when the question is asked. Give ten seconds thinking time and get everybody to move to their corners at the same time. Expect to have to encourage them to speed up with a saying like: "Move it, move, move, move and move people!"

- **ABCD Corners and Cards Together**
  - This is a good strategy for avoiding copying. The teacher must not tell the students exactly what is being done, otherwise it won't work.
  - Get the students to put the correct answer from their ABCD cards in their pockets. Now, get them to move to the right ABCD corner in the room.
  - Ask them to put their cards in the air whilst they are at their ABCD corner all at the same time. If there is difference between the corners they have moved to and their card, the teacher will be able to ascertain this immediately.
  - If there is a difference, the student has changed their mind since they picked their card. This could mean they have been copying or rethought their answer. Therefore, it warrants further questioning by the teacher whilst the rest of the class are directed to their main tasks.

True or False

This is a question which has a true or false (yes or no is also an alternative) answer, hence the T/F cards in the AfL Box. The key here is to make the true or false answers so similar that the question is challenging. The students put up the required T or F card much like ABCD, all at the same time.

Quick tip

Why not make it even easier? First thing at the start of the year, get the students to put a huge colourful "T" and an "F" in the back two pages of their book. No resources required at all.

Mexican Wave, Teacher Style

Line up the students at the back of class, and if they agree with a statement on the whiteboard, then they stand up like a Mexican wave. If they disagree, then they hunch down like a ball. Students who are unsure can go from a small Mexican wave to a standing ball shape repeatedly over a few seconds. The statement should be related to the learning needed to progress onto the next part of the lesson. The Mexican wave should indicate that they are either really thinking about it or unsure, either of which warrants further questioning by the teacher.

Circular Questioning

Get the students to stand up for ease, or this task can be done sitting down, if they need to wake up a little. This has adaptations where the answer is a direction. For example: N, NE, E, SE, S, SW, W, NW if you are doing a geography lesson or forces when doing physics, including up, down, right, and left.

Conduct the assessment very much like the Mexican wave, by getting the students to push both hands in a particular direction according to their answer. This can be left and right or down or up or for directions that indicate where north is for the students.

Students love it, and people will walk past seeing the children doing what seems like dancing. It is easy to spot where people are incorrect or unsure, as they will not fit the pattern of the moving class as long as they all move at the same time.

Fists and Fingers

This is basically a version of using one, two, three, or four with fingers to choose multiple choice answers with a twist. Students put their fists out right in front of their body whilst the teacher reads out a multiple choice set of answers. The teacher then counts down from five to zero for thinking time; at zero the students stick out the number of fingers for the correct answer. Don't be afraid of one finger or two finger gestures; humour is often the best way to deal with it. By starting with fists for the thinking time, most copying is also eliminated as long as all answers come out simultaneously.

Coloured Cards of any Description

Coloured cards are great just to mix it up. Ask the multiple choice question with answers related to different colours. Colours can be given any meaning or perhaps link them to a font colour being used. The best way is linking them to the subject, for example, when artists are linking colours to mood. Most subjects can have colours associated with them, so think of a subject and get some coloured cards made to mix the assessment up.

ActiVote

This software is attached to the Promethean whiteboard technology, although it can be used with ActivStudio or the new ActivInspire without an interactive whiteboard. It is a pod-shaped keypad and works much like *Who Wants to Be a Millionaire: Ask the Audience*. It is superior because it delivers information on which students got it wrong, along with various other useful statistics. The only issue is timings in terms of getting the hardware in and out. However, it can be done very quickly in a well-practiced class. So, as with everything else, get the children to do it and practice doing it regularly every six to eight lessons.

Quick tip

If there is access to a class set of tablets, then this can be done with several different apps, such as Quizzam or Socrative. Try out the different ones if you are one of the lucky ones whose school has great IT infrastructure.

Chapter 7:

DIFFERENTIATION TECHNIQUES

Differentiation is a key theme discussed throughout this book and is absolutely essential in an outstanding lesson. For a lesson to be outstanding, learning must be differentiated and promote independence and collaboration as an underlying theme. In this chapter we will discuss various differentiation strategies that lend themselves to this purpose. Each strategy can be used to build variety in lessons and an expectation of progress and achievement amongst all students.

Differentiation by Task

This is the simplest form of differentiation; just give out different tasks based upon the differentiated learning objectives.

Consider what the higher achievers should understand by the end of the lesson. This technique works best in mixed ability classes and is often facilitated by different worksheets with differing levels of language.

Different Starting Points

This works particularly well on any closed-question-based subject such as maths. Imagine there are ten questions on a worksheet or in a text book that are gradually increasing in difficulty but on the same theme (e.g. quadratic equations).

A typical lesson would include lower-ability students doing the earlier simpler questions (1-3); middle-ability students doing the intermediate difficulty (4-6); and the higher-ability students doing the latter questions (7-10).

Differentiated Success Criteria

Here is an opportunity to use success criteria to differentiate in lesson. What is the desired outcome from students?

For example, lower abilities must include at least three keywords and higher abilities must contain at least seven (discussed in the literacy section). This can expand and link with all different types of tasks. Consider another example where you are creating a revision worksheet on a unit of work. This uses Bloom's Taxonomy and some simple literacy objectives:

- Higher abilities must justify their statements using complex sentences.
- Lower ability must state the problems and explain using compound sentences.

Hints and Tips

For the task, make a set of hints and tips in envelopes or on the front desk. Set the task and allow the students to use the hints before they ask the teacher. This means they are learning to rely upon themselves and not the teacher. Just make sure there is positive encouragement to use the hints and tips when they have explored their brain, book, or buddy (3B4Me). Often, many students challenge themselves regardless of ability and don't open the hints and tips.

Don't Tell Them What to Do: Discovery

This works well in any experimental scenario. Imagine testing whether weight affects friction with your class of nine-year-olds. The more able students will just get the materials and discuss how to test whether mass affects friction. A middle-ability student may have hints and tips given to them, whereas the lower abilities will have hints and tips and work with a teaching assistant to guide them through the process.

Teaching Assistants (TA)

Teaching assistants are a godsend, especially to those mixed-ability classes with very low and very high abilities. In an outstanding lesson, the teaching assistant is informed of the learning taking place prior to the lesson. This allows them the time to have a clear focus on the skills they are trying to develop in that class. For example, what key questions are being asked when a TA is available to work with specific students?

- What learning focus is being given to the TA?
- What students are working the TA?
- What kind of questions is the TA asking?

- Has there been a discussion between the TA and the teacher on what works well with the children with which they are working? Is it illustrations, keywords, analogies, number lines, or anything else? They often know this information, which is invaluable for the teacher in helping to get to know a child.
- Communicate with the TA and make sure there is feedback on the students during, and possibly after, the lesson.

There is no doubt that TAs are a great way of introducing differentiation in the form of help and guidance. So, when designing differentiated tasks, think how the TA can help the learning. Teachers can find it very useful to have a plan in place for certain students over the term or half-term. This can come in the form of support planners, which cover all of the key questions above and allow the TA and teacher to be at their most effective for that child or group of children.

The Matrix

Matrix problems are where students find their own paths through selecting learning pathways. In simple terms, this could be a mixture of different sums or questions on a play or practical exercise. The important thing is that the students choose their path depending on the teacher's subtle influence and the student's own decision. Below are two different ways of executing matrix activities using some other differentiation tips in combination:

1. **Matrix with Hint and Tips and Self-Assessment**
   ◦ Write down or print a series of differentiated questions on the lesson topic (make sure they are at the top of the pieces of paper). Now fold them in half with the questions at the front and write/print a hint or tip at the back. Number each question according to its difficulty. For example, one being a straight forward recall question, and five being a super challenging creation or evaluation question. There are two ways to then carry out the activity:

     ▪ Aim for the students to get as many points as possible making it a competition. This means that to get the highest points total, they must attempt the higher-numbered questions and, therefore, challenge themselves.

     ▪ Another way is to set each person a target point level. An example would be a lower-ability student may get eleven and a higher-ability student may get sixteen. However, this overtly points out who is the more intelligent child. This is something to avoid as it is a really negative message. A way of getting around it to set a target of fifteen points, then instruct higher-ability students to get at least two level four questions; middle-ability students to get three level three questions; and lower-ability students to get at least one level three question. Although this still sets different tasks, it is less overt and works well.

Quick tip

To make this even more student-centred and independent, why not allow the students to self-assess or peer-assess each other's answers in a matrix activity? The teacher is then free to circulate through the class and help students group by group or individually. Just make sure the class is trustworthy and so will not be tempted to look at the answers before completing the question.

2. *Matrix-Move Across the Descriptors*
   ◦ Have a series of descriptors ready to use. This is basically a list of small tasks. The tasks vary in difficulty by using Bloom's Taxonomy (e.g. state, explain, justify). The students can choose their own starting points and work their way across the descriptors like Blockbusters, an old quiz game. They choose their own path again, based upon the teacher's guidance.

A matrix can be a lot of preparation, but it is well worth it if they are used repeatedly. However, teachers are busy, so there may not be time to immediately make one. No problem: create the matrix activity by simply using a question and answer book and picking the relevant questions. This involves hardly any preparation at all and is still effective if the questions are numbered according to their difficulty.

Circus and Carousel Activities

Set up different activities, usually practical, around the room where students change task every time according to the teacher's timings. The timeframe may be anywhere from one to four minutes for each change of activity depending on how many have been set up.

Each activity can be differentiated with different questions and/or hints and tips. The most effective are where the circus/carousel involves kinaesthetic activities and learning-related challenges within that practical context.

In an outstanding lesson there always has to be something the teacher can challenge a child with, which is often hidden in their back pocket. In a circus/carousel activity, a simple way to add this extension is to place it in a central island with the rest of the activities around the outside.

So, for the challenge, students can opt out of the carousel for one cycle (one to four minutes) and visit the central island(s) where there are super-challenging activities displayed. Make it clear that everyone is expected to try the challenge if they are successful in some or all of the questions around the outside. It is possible not all will succeed, but the important thing is to try.

Tarsia

Tarsia allows teachers to create a wide range of jigsaws, dominos, and follow-me activities using a program freely available to download on the Internet via www.mmlsoft.com/hdata/tarsia_home.php.

Select the type of activity and input as many questions and answers as needed. The software is built for mathematical operations; however, it can suit any subject. It supports the uploading of images and allows the checking of the answers on the table screen. It then prints out the jumbled up version for the students or the solution.

It is also very visual, as the teacher does not tell the students the final jigsaw shape. They may be aiming for a pentagon or hexagon or octagon, but don't tell them.

Tarsia activities promote group work and discussion, and are far more engaging than standard questions out of a textbook. They are an ideal way to revise or consolidate a topic and different-shaped Tarsias can be created in order to differentiate by writing questions of varying difficulty. Observations of the students are simple, since when they are complete, the shape will appear and the sense of satisfaction they get will be clear to see.

There are many ways to make Tarsias more challenging and to differentiate them:

- **Answer Repetition**—Make sure at least a couple of the answers are the same. This makes it even harder for students to complete the puzzle by luck alone, as they will get the wrong shape of the jigsaw.

- **Leave Parts Blank**—Pick a few cards for the more able students from your Tarsia and don't write the answers or the question. Students will then have to fill the question or answers in for themselves.

- **Deliberate Mistakes**—Put some deliberate mistakes in the Tarsia to test the students. Make a decision about whether to tell them there are mistakes; it may be appropriate to tell or to keep it secret for more of a challenge, depending on the student's confidence. Once a student finds the mistakes, make sure he or she corrects them.

- **Revision Lessons**—Get students to create Tarsia puzzles themselves on their various revision topics. Get the other students to complete their Tarisa depending on their revision needs. This produces a bank of Tarsias to use in different classes. Just make sure they are checked thoroughly before they are used.

Writing Frames

Writing frames, as already discussed in the literacy section, are merely a start or structure to the students' learning, very much like the TASC wheel already discussed. This can include instructions to use certain sentence starters, verbs and/or a set of titles to follow to write any form of extended writing such as a report. The differentiation comes from some students being given the structure; whereas, more able students will be given less guidance.

Differentiated Roles

The Teacher

Why should teachers teach all the time when the students can do it? By teaching, students can become empowered and more confident, developing many wider learning skills. Learning retention according to Maine Laboratories is 90 per cent if the subject is taught to others, so what a great reason to involve students teaching in a lesson.

Students teaching others can also include leading, teamwork, developing explanations, and working to reshape learning. Think of how difficult it is for an adult to teach—so what better challenge for a child?

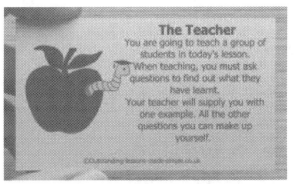

To give a student the task, the teacher differentiation card can be used as a simple delivery tool where no major explanation is needed.

Allowing the students to teach, however, can be a difficult lesson to plan. Here are a couple of lesson structures incorporating the student teacher to help in planning.

Plan A: Student Teachers

This is a lesson structure where features of the Outstanding Lesson Framework become clear. Three or more separate elements are taught (e.g. three types of poems in English; three separate principles in science; three different areas of physiology in physical education).

1. Split the learning into three discrete parts. Get the majority of the class to do some preparatory questions that will help them achieve the three main learning objectives.

2. Differentiate immediately by selecting three higher-ability students to become student teachers. Give the students the teacher card with a resource for their subject area to teach, such as a text book or different worksheets.

3. Discuss the learning with the student teachers and confirm their learning by asking a hinge point question. Now indicate overtly clear success criteria (e.g. you must teach x, y, and z within . . . minutes).

4. Instruct the student teachers to do their own Assessment for Learning (hinge point style) which confirms the learning in their peers. If necessary, give them some questions to get them started.

5. As the student teachers are preparing themselves, arrange the rest of the class into three groups. Teach some background on the subject to be taught and give out clear success criteria to the main group and the following instructions:

    ◦ All three groups must visit each student teacher in a rotation.
    ◦ The teacher will say "change", or any other keyword to cause groups to move in a clockwise direction to the next student teacher.
    ◦ Students can make any notes they wish during the lesson, but instruct that there is to be no copying.

6. The student teachers teach their groups and rotate so everybody in the main groups has been taught all three areas.

7. Role reversal: After this process, student teachers only understand their subject (one of three covered in the lesson). Now each group must teach their student teacher the other two sections covered. This is the most challenging section for the student teachers as they have to learn two sections quickly and the other students have to teach what they have learned.

8. At the end of the lesson the teacher assesses the whole group to confirm the learning and make any interventions necessary.

Plan B: Student Teachers

1. Identify the main learning objective (e.g. We are learning to multiply fractions).

2. Get the majority of the class to do some preparatory questions that will help them achieve the main learning objectives.

3. Whilst they are doing the questions, pick out six student teachers with the cards. Student teachers can have varied abilities and it is often effective using the most disruptive, because once they are given responsibility, they tend to thrive.

4. Teach the student teachers the skill or technique to be taught to the main class and ask a hinge point-style question to check their understanding.

5. Share the clear success criteria with the student teachers (e.g. you must teach x, y, and z in . . . minutes).

6. Instruct the student teachers to do their own Assessment for Learning (hinge point style), which confirms the learning in their peers. If necessary, give them some questions to get them started.

7. As the student teachers are finishing off preparing to teach, arrange the class by splitting them into six groups and do the following:

   ◦ Assign each group a student teacher.
   ◦ They are given . . . minutes to teach their subject using the resources given such as, a MWB to teach with or anything practical related to the subject.

8. During the activity, visit all of the groups at least once, however, only interfere if they are off track. In a successful student teacher lesson, the students will normally get on without the teachers help, resulting in true independence.

9. After the time is up, stop the class and remove the teachers to the front and assess all using a plenary technique.

Quick tip

Add a bit of competition to keep up the pace and engagement. Set a few questions as a plenary to each group to determine the best teacher. By letting the student teachers know at the start, they will try to give their best. The pleasant surprise is that the best teacher is often not the brightest student.

The Assessor

The Assessor is the differentiation card given to a student at the start of the lesson. It informs them that they must assess someone else's work and give feedback during the lesson. The teacher can control this by giving the nod when the time is appropriate.

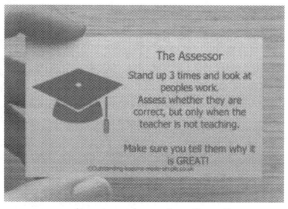

Varying who receives the card across the class will build up the confidence of the students slowly but surely. It may be necessary to give guidance on assessing sometimes and at other times not, it all depends on the students. Why not try coupling it with student-friendly success criteria to make it even more effective and simple for the student to grasp.

The Celebrator

The Celebrator differentiation card is given to a student at the start of the lesson. As with the Assessor card, it instructs them to assess someone else's work with a twist. The student with the card gives detailed feedback to the teacher on who they think has done the best work, and most importantly, why.

The teacher can then write a note in the assessed student's homework diary/planner, or give their parent a ring to tell them their child's work has been exemplary. By getting the student to explain why the work is good, the teacher is making the students justify their opinions and link to evidence. This is a key higher order learning objective for students and, therefore, a great way to differentiate.

The Chair

The Chair is a differentiation card given to a student at the start of the lesson, which includes an overall decision to be made and justified. The person given the Chair card will decide on an outcome after hearing a debate or discussion on a problem posed by the teacher. This is a good challenge for higher abilities, since again, it uses higher-order thinking skills. To make this a group activity, have the chair as the leader in a committee that makes the overall decision.

The Aide

Of all the differentiation cards described in this chapter, it is important to note that more than one can be given out in a lesson, since this means more differentiation. The Aide differentiation card is usually given to a student who is very comfortable with their learning, but may need to improve their social skills by interacting with others. The Aide facilitates this by getting the student to help explain to their peers how to attempt questions. This is done in a way which the teacher controls and, therefore, the child is not blamed by their peers for interfering in their work.

Problem Anyone? I Can Help.

This is a poster which allows students to place their queries up at any time so the teacher can address them in class or individually. Teachers have to be approachable; however, at the same time, they are very busy beings, so sometimes it can be hard for a student to approach them. By making "Problem anyone? I can help!" posters (below), this allows the teacher to get feedback whether in or out of the classroom.

It is important to ensure that all students feel safe and confident enough to provide feedback, so sometimes two posters can be more effective. Consider one that the students place their names on and another which is anonymous. If the anonymous poster is used, there may be far more feedback from the students in classes where there are some very shy people. Just put up these posters with a pack of sticky notes underneath and let their queries be posted up.

Place any questions on the notes underneath with
your name on the note.
Place the note on the poster.
Notes are removed daily and discussed next lesson.

Place any questions on the post-it notes
underneath.
No name is needed.
Place it on this poster as notes are removed
daily and discussed next lesson.

Class Poster Suggestions: The one on the left is where the students write their name and the one on the right is where students can be anonymous.

Can Other Students Help?

This poster is to aid the students collaborating with each other either inside or outside of the lesson. The poster is in the same format as "Problem anyone? I can help!" However, the students choose to respond to the questions placed. It will be slow going at first, but once it has been used, a lot of it will work brilliantly. The students will become more resilient and learn to rely on each other as well as themselves. In terms of vertical tutor groups (multiple year groups in one tutor group), this is also a fantastic way to get students interacting. It helps by encouraging students to post their unanswered questions on the board, and encouraging the older members of the tutor group to help answer them.

Underneath is a suggestion for a tutor group poster. This one is for a tutor group where they answer each other's questions every Friday:

Place any questions on the post-it notes underneath
with your name.
Place it on this poster and another student will pick
one to answer each Friday.

Quick tip Why not use the Aide card with this? Give the card to a student and ask them to choose some questions to help with from the poster.

Chapter 8:
PEER- AND SELF-ASSESSMENT

Combining peer-assessment (assessing others) and/or self-assessment (assessing themselves) into a lesson plan is always a good idea. This allows the students to own their learning and cement that independent feel within the classroom. Be aware that the aim when doing peer—or self-assessment is to make it much more informative than just giving the answers out.

Within the Outstanding Lesson Framework, peer—or self-assessment comes after the differentiation phase; however, it can be entwined throughout the lesson and should be closely linked with success criteria. The success criteria allow the students to assess themselves and realise what learning they have achieved. Therefore, the writing of success criteria is essential and a vitally important part of self—or peer-assessment. Once students are used to assessing themselves, they will do this without thinking, and this kind of evaluative practice will continue to make them a lifelong learner.

For learning to be the focus, students should be taking ownership and, therefore, know how to improve it. So here are some methods to carry out this type of assessment that could be placed directly into an outstanding lesson:

Checklist

Students are given a set checklist of aims or success criteria that they need to achieve. The checklist is then used by the students to assess each other or themselves. The vitally important thing is that these success criteria are not merely answers but a guide to raising the quality of their answers.

Mark Schemes

Mark schemes are checklists for test preparation. They allow the students to compare their answers in preparation for external examinations. The key here is to use the schemes to improve answers not just to say the answer is wrong.

This is a fantastic opportunity to use the highlighters in the AfL box. Students use the highlighters to either peer—or self-assessment answers. Green is used to highlight the correctly worded section that gets the marks, and orange is used for wording that is nearly correct but currently gets no marks. Pink can be used for incorrect (it is more positive than red).

Quick tip

Checklists or mark schemes can be made into group activities by allowing students to find someone with a correct (green) answer to help them improve their incorrect (orange/pink) answer.

Make sure any improvements are in a different coloured pen so the students can see the right answer when they revisit their work.

It is also important to not allow students to read other's answers; just allow the correct answers to guide the incorrect.

Students Developing Their Own Tests

Students analyse their own weaknesses using a Mark Scheme and produce a test based upon their weak areas. Developing the test can be the main task of the lesson in some cases, which is combined with the teacher taking small groups to help them grasp any content that was a struggle. The students are then challenged to create their own exam and a structured Mark Scheme on those areas.

Model Answers

Give students model answers for a type of question. This allows them to structure their answers in the same way and see the techniques used. They can use this to see the possible areas of improvement for their own answers. If it is taken one step further, students can design their own model in groups to create answers to specified problems.

Why Is This a B, A, F?

Analyse answers that are given a specific grade, or maybe a mark out ten. Get the students to determine using a mark scheme or success criteria based on why the work should or shouldn't be awarded this mark.

Mark This

Students are given pieces of work to mark by the teacher. Try starting in stages, for example, initially blind (no mark scheme) and then give out the mark schemes to individuals, or the whole class depending on how they are doing.

Quick tip
To differentiate, give out different answers to different abilities. Brighter students can be given a more difficult answer to complete (usually varying in the level of literacy and/or how close the answer is to the right one). The aim of the task is then to improve the work to a set level according to that student's target.

Best Answer

Give students three or more different areas to research based around a topic. Group students together who have studied the three different areas and give them a question based on the topic. Next, they collaboratively come up with the best answer to the question, which must include all three areas. This can be further developed by getting students to compare their key points within groups. The teacher collaborates with the class to produce a whole-class answer to the question. The key is then to develop everybody's individual answers to the high standard after the group answer is done.

Mark the Comment

This works really well in a class where there are sometimes silly comments or a class where they struggle to focus. Students assess each other's work according to success criteria using a Post-it note. The students rotate work and the next person marks the comment, not the work. The students states if the comment allows the work to be improved. If it cannot, they improve the comment. All silly comments disappear.

Two Stars and a Question/Wish

The teaching idea here is to get the students to mark each other's work using either two stars and a wish or two stars and a question. Many people will have heard of two stars and a wish: two positive comments are given on a piece of work and one area given to improve. Two stars and a question involves two positive comments and a question for the student based upon the area that needs development.

Both techniques involve students asking questions of each other, thereby developing their collaborative skills, questioning, and resilience. Students will think harder, and some will attempt to make a very difficult question and others a simple one. The teacher's job is to engineer things so the pitch and groupings are right for all. This can be done by using hints and tips with some common questions as starters to help the students out.

Chapter 9:
PLENARY AND RESHAPING AFTERWARDS

In simplest terms, the plenary is just a summary of the lesson in which there are key questions that need to be answered. But what is the key question to focus on for the teacher? Here are some examples:

What have the children learned?

What skills have they developed?

How does this impact the next lesson plan?

It all sounds complicated, so draw this back to simplicity. All of these questions can be considered when talking about the learning objectives and success criteria. Success of the lesson can be judged depending upon whether the children have achieved the learning objectives and/or the success criteria.

In its simplest form, just ask the students questions based upon the learning objectives or success criteria. This way, the teacher knows where everybody is in their learning and allows time for intervention and further help if necessary.

There are two simple ways of developing a plenary. The first type is much like the hinge point question discussed earlier in Chapter 6 and the second being metacognition. Each type will be considered in this chapter.

What Is a Hinge Point Plenary?

This is the simplest plenary and perhaps the quickest. Any of the hinge point question strategies can be used by asking a few questions at the end of the lesson based upon the differentiated learning objectives. Try this process:

- Refer back to the learning objectives or success criteria.

- Ask a question on each differentiated learning objective.

- If the pitch wasn't quite right and the class achieves lower or higher than expected, just have a couple of easier or harder questions prepared.

This process allows the teacher to know the capability and achievement of all the students. If there is time, some final intervention can take place.

What Is a Metacognitive Plenary?

We are all aware that the plenary is a vital part of every lesson, but it is generally reported to be the most difficult phase, usually due to lack of time. If the lesson is planned well and there is time, then try a metacognitive plenary or a plenary involving "knowing about knowing".

In a metacognitive plenary, students are asked to develop the ability to think and talk about their learning. This illustrates their awareness of what they have learned and also how they have learned it—this is true metacognition.

Designing a Metacognitive Plenary

Metacognitive plenaries can be used to train the students to use suggested strategies for learning or for problem solving. Another important aspect, which teachers may have heard about is metamemory, which is defined as "knowing about memory and mnemonic strategies". These skills are important for any child's individual learning. Students need to build up the repertoire of skills they use to learn with, whether it be mind maps, Logovisual tools, concept mapping, note revision, mnemonics, or reading and application skills.

Here we give some examples of how two metacognitive approaches may be used in a simple way. However, the first two things to decide are:

Who is leading this, the teacher or the students?

Can the students lead?

It is always better for the students to lead, but, in some classes, the teacher may decide they have to take more of the lead role.

The next step is to prepare in advance the right type of questions into simple categories such as:

- Describe the type of learning in which you participated.

- Describe how your learning went. Could it be improved? How?

The two types described above can all start with one of the 5 Ws (Who? What? When? Where? Why?), or add How (5Ws/H), plus other keywords. As long as these words are used to start the questions, then the metacognitive plenary will be effective and probing. Here are some examples of question types to get the design started.

Describe What Type of Learning in Which You Participated

- How were techniques/activities used in class to tackle problems?
- How were specific parts of the learning process used?
- Who led? Who helped the team focus? How did each role help the team learn?

Describe How Your Learning Went

Could It Be Improved? How?

This is the time to initiate thinking of different viewpoints or areas. Learning problems in the lesson can be approached in different ways in order to improve them. With practice, students can be relied upon to have a bank of questions in their arsenal ready to begin to assess fairly and critically each other's thinking. The questions naturally lead onto higher-order thinking such as, evaluation of their learning in the lesson ("Could it be improved?" and "How?"). As well as the 5 Ws/H, these questions may begin with:

- But . . .

- Did you have a plan or a strategy? Did it work well?

- Have you thought of different methods of learning for this challenge?

- What did you think about? Why?

- Imagine you were looking from a different perspective, what would you think?

All of these questions are very generic, so use them as a basis of question development for the subject-specific lesson. By using them, students are being prompted to consider how they are thinking as well as if they have employed their learning techniques in the lesson, which will serve them in any other context.

Quick tip
Metacognitive plenaries can be done easily without much preparation. Just create a learning log for a student's book. Pick a few key questions (e.g. "What did you learn?", "How did you learn it?", and "What could have improved?"). Structure can be in the form of a pyramid or columns. Columns have the added bonus that they can be reused in different lessons, and there is clear evidence in the books for progression.

"Hinge Point" Plenaries:
For When You Are Running Out of Time

In lessons, we need plenaries that require a little time and techniques in the back pocket, which take no preparation. Some of these techniques are meant to be reminders of the hinge point questions. For a fuller explanation, please refer to Chapter 6. Try these out:

Circular Questioning

For questions which have a definitive direction as an answer (e.g. north/south/east/west or up/down/left/right). Ask the students to point in the correct direction to answer the differentiated questions based on your learning objectives.

Exit Questions

Students are asked a question on the board which they answer on Post-it notes and give to the teacher on the way out of the classroom. Make sure the answer to the question is easy to interpret since this means when they leave the classroom, it is simple to mentally note the issues and use it to plan next lesson.

Split the Board Using Differentiated Questions

Have multiple questions on the boards aimed at your different learning objectives. Ask students to choose their chosen success criteria. This might be their target grade which is shown on the question. Get them to place their name on the Post-it note with their answer and either assess quickly in lesson, or just use it for the next lesson, if time is running out.

Connect the Pictures to the Learning

Ask the students to identify which picture identifies learning the most in the lesson, the pictures can be anything. Just make sure that there is a more obscure version for your high abilities which requires more articulate explanation and wider-thinking skills. The students must explain why.

Self-Assessing or Peer-Assessing

Any self—or peer-assessing strategies can be used as a plenary because they allow the students to know what they have learned and how well they are doing. But be aware, only do this if the class is trained well and there are clear learning objectives and success criteria for the students to comprehend. If there is any doubt, the teacher should run the plenary until the students are used to assessing using metacognition, learning objective and/or success criteria.

Learning Logs

As mentioned, there are a plethora of learning logs on the Internet which, in their simplest form, talk about what students have learned, and in their most cognitive, become a metacognitive plenary. Integrating this in all lessons is as simple as putting a page in their book which just says, "What have I learned today?" After each lesson, they fill in the table as their summary. To develop this further, just introduce extra questions such as "How have you learned today?" and "What is the next thing you would like to learn?"

Washing Line

The washing line technique is a good way to show progress in the lesson using a bit of old string, pegs, and some paper. Follow the steps below:

- When planning the lesson, ensure the differentiated learning objectives are clear and linked to grades, where possible.

- Mark the washing line with the levels in order of difficulty. For example, further down the washing line, the difficulty of the learning objectives rises.

- Explain clearly to the students displaying the learning objectives and success criteria.

- At the beginning of the lesson, students put their initials on a piece of paper and attach it to the washing line with a peg at the level they are at right now.

- Later on in the lesson, or at the plenary, students must move their marker to where they believe they are at currently.

This shows clear progression in a very visual way for the students.

Quick tip

Remember to link ideas. In this case, the washing line can be combined with a metacognitive plenary. Students can explain how and/or why they were able to learn the learning objective.

Target Circles

The target circle is an adaptation of the washing line. The same thing is done, but this time, different sized circles are drawn as in the diagram on the right. Essentially, like a dart board, each area has a learning objective or success criteria associated with it. Students can use Post-it notes with initials on them to label where they are at the beginning, and then when the plenary is done, they repeat the exercise. They then draw an arrow between their two points showing progression.

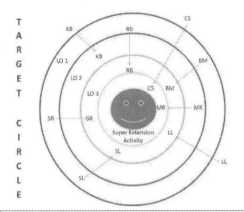

Target circle using a small group of students where "LO" means the differentiated learning objectives one, two, and three. In this case, the teacher has also added an extension activity. As you can see, progression is clear.

Quick tip

Want to do this with very little preparation? Just draw the target circles on a whiteboard and get the students to come up and write their initials on the whiteboard. They then draw the arrows to connect where they started to where they have ended in their learning. This is super quick and easy, and it only requires using whiteboard pens from the AfL box.

Ranking

Rank anything in the key learning objectives in order of importance. This may be holistic and done on mini-whiteboards so the teacher can observe easily where the students are at currently. If a lesson is prop led, then use the prop for a more physical finish.

Drawings and Sketches

This can be done in any lesson. Students draw a sketch to sum up the lesson. In a plenary, it is important that the teacher can clearly see what is going on, so the drawing can be done in books or on a mini-whiteboard, or it can be required as an answer to an exit question.

Keywords

Use the keyword bank from the lesson collated by the teacher. The students' feedback individually or in groups to sum up the lesson in terms of keywords they have learned. Students then write a summary of the learning using those keywords. Be aware though, the whole class is not easily assessed, but the teacher can use group feedback or peer-assessment ideas to complete the assessment. Even better, this technique can be combined with the homework task (e.g. using the keywords to complete the writing of a concept map).

Plenaries: A Summary

To sum up the important points:

- Don't leave too little time for the plenary.

- Keep some simple questions in the back pocket using your AfL toolbox to facilitate this.

- Experiment. Any teaching strategy can be used in a plenary as long as it is based upon either the students or the teacher assessing the students' learning.

- Don't restrict these important points just to this chapter. Many techniques can be used as a plenary, so explore any chapter of this book, and hopefully, be inspired.

Chapter 10:

HOMEWORK

This is a short but necessary section. Homework, aka home learning, has three main objectives:

- To consolidate the learning in the lesson

- To feed into the next lesson if there is a running theme (e.g. in the middle of a unit of work)

- To prepare students for new learning in the next lesson, such as
  - open-ended research;
  - directed research;
  - students teaching themselves using prepared resources and self-assessment ("The Flipped Classroom": see below) usually on a virtual learning environment (VLE).

Almost all techniques throughout the book can be used as a homework activity. Just adapt the ideas already discussed to design a homework activity. To start the imagination, here are just a few examples:

- Concept maps

- Student developing tests and mark schemes

- Students learning summaries using Pictionary-style exercises

- Metacognitive or metamemory tasks

- Crossword production from keywords

To think of homework, just go through the book and pick out a technique.

The Flipped Classroom: The Future?

The "flipped classroom" is presently a hot topic of conversation in the educational community. The flipped classroom could be a book in itself; however, here we provide an opening view to the discussion and how it may link to the Outstanding Lesson Framework.

It is useful to describe the concept in simple terms. All lessons follow a rough format known as TEMP, which stands for:

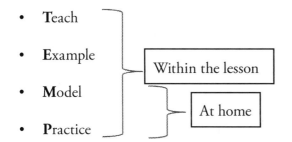

- **T**each

- **E**xample

- **M**odel

- **P**ractice

Within the lesson

At home

All teachers **t**each some new knowledge, often using an **e**xample, which is then **m**odelled in a particular context. The students are then given time to **p**ractice. In an outstanding lesson, we seek to emphasise the **p**, or the **p**ractice, since that is where the learning takes place. Throughout this book and in the Outstanding Lesson Framework, **p**ractice is the determining factor for a successful lesson. In the Framework, most of the **p**ractice by the students is in the differentiation phase after the hinge point question.

The challenge in planning lessons using the Framework is to plan the teaching episodes so that adequate time is given for students to **p**ractice. This is often the toughest skill for a teacher, and this is where flipping the classroom changes the emphasis.

In the flipped classroom model, the **t**eaching, **e**xample, and the **m**odelling of the learning can be done before the lesson as homework. This allows more of the lesson to be done since **p**ractice means less didactic or chalk-and-talk-style teaching and more independent learning from students. So when flipping the classroom, the **TEMP** model changes slightly:

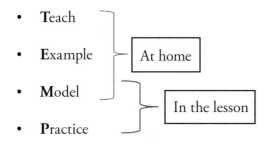

- **T**each

- **E**xample

- **M**odel

- **P**ractice

At home

In the lesson

For flipping the classroom to work, it has to be well structured with a good basis in the VLE of the school. Students also need to be able to teach and assess themselves at home, which requires input from the teacher in producing detailed materials and resources.

Students can be taught independently through a variety of mediums such as online tutorials in the form of worksheets, videos, and PowerPoints.

Quick tip

For free access to an expansive set of online videos on many different subjects and levels, visit The Kahn Academy (www.khanacademy.org). Also look for different apps for subjects that post online videos such as Mathswatch. For those who prefer to write their own material, have a look at Educreations, Showbie, and Explain Everything where teachers can write lessons online for students to access from home.

How Does Flipping the Classroom and the Framework Fit Together?

In the Framework, there are no timings, since this is up to the teacher in their planning. The premise of the Framework is only to outline the important features of an outstanding lesson and put them in a chronological order as a starting point. As teachers, we progress and change during our career, and with that, the Framework should dissolve as creativity and innovation becomes more endemic.

Sections can move around and appear in different orders. For example, does the hinge point have to be twenty minutes into the lesson or can it be as a starter? When flipping the classroom, it may be necessary to assess everyone closer to the beginning of the lesson. This is so the lesson can be pitched effectively based on evidence straight from the students' feedback. In the flipped lesson, the learning will still need to be described, the teacher will still need to teach, and will need to assess, and allow students to assess their own learning.

So the simple answer is that the only difference is that the initial timings will be probably shorter in a flipped lesson. This allows that more time will be available for students to work, and for the teacher to walk around and help them. Flipping the classroom is a simple but innovative approach, and coupled with the Framework, outstanding learning is only a small step away.

TEACHING AFTER THE FRAMEWORK

The vision when designing the Outstanding Lesson Framework was that it should be seen as a beginning to lesson design and not the end. The aim is to allow teachers to decipher the lesson planning ambiguity in the teaching profession and give clear guidance on how to do it simply.

Therefore, the chronological approach to structuring lessons in the Framework is a stepping stone and essentially a list of important features that create outstanding learning in a classroom and not the end of the learning journey.

Once there is confidence in all the techniques of the Outstanding Lesson Framework, then really start experimenting, keeping the features of the Framework in mind. As mentioned before throughout the book, jumble it up and see where the planning takes you, keeping in mind the most important feature: progress for all students in the class.

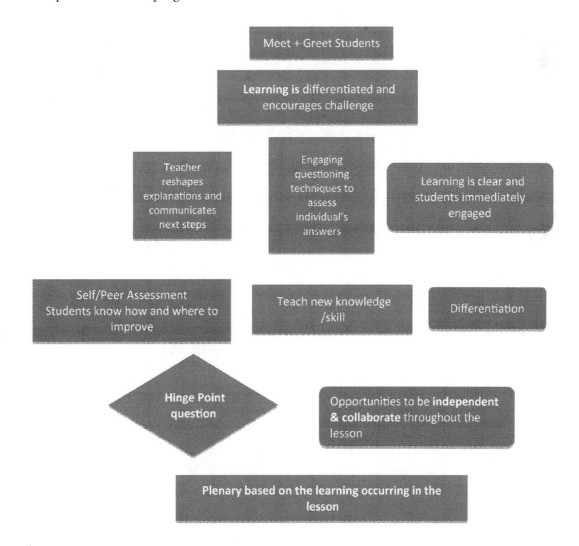

The Outstanding Lesson Framework simplified further and jumbled up? What lesson can you plan now?